This book is to be returned
the day date st

£7.95

THE MUSIC 𝄞ℒ

WRITING TOGETHER
THE SONGWRITER'S GUIDE TO COLLABORATION

Walter Carter

UNIVERSITY OF LIVERPOOL
DEPARTMENT OF CONTINUING EDUCATION LIBRARY

Omnibus Press
London/New York/Sydney

62.113

First published 1988 by Writer's Digest Books, Cincinnati, Ohio, USA

© Walter Carter
This edition © Copyright 1990 Omnibus Press
(A Division of Book Sales Limited)

Edited by Chris Barstow

Text Art Direction AB3

Cover Designed by Pearce Marchbank

Cover photo by Julian Hawkins

ISBN 0.7119.1713.2

Order No: OP 45103

All rights reserved. No part of this book may be reproduced in any form or by any electronic or mechanical means, including information storage or retrieval systems, without permission in writing from the publisher, except by a reviewer who may quote brief passages.

Exclusive distributors:
Book Sales Limited,
8/9 Frith Street,
London W1V 5TZ, UK.

Music Sales Corporation,
225 Park Avenue South,
New York, NY 10003, USA.

Music Sales Pty Limited,
120 Rothschild Avenue,
Rosebery, NSW 2018, Australia.

To the Music Trade only:
Music Sales Limited,
8/9 Frith Street,
London W1V 5TZ, UK.

Typeset by Wakeworth
Printed in England by
St. Edmundsbury Press,
Bury St. Edmunds, Suffolk.

CONTENTS

ACKNOWLEDGMENTS

A great number of people have contributed to this book, but I would particularly like to thank the songwriters – Pat Bunch, Roger Greenaway, Will Jennings, Mary Ann Kennedy, Dave Loggins, Dennis Morgan, Bob Morrison and Pam Rose – who took the time away from their writing to be interviewed. A special thanks goes to Jay Livingston, whose songwriting stories I would rather be listening to now.

An equally valuable contribution was made by all the songwriters I have written with through the years; they provided me with the experiences that comprise the core of this book.

Finally, my wife Christie and my six-year-old stepson Beau deserve a special word of thanks. Christie never tried to drag me off to a film when I had to work, and Beau only once demanded equal time on the computer to play games. For this I am deeply grateful.

INTRODUCTION

Cole Porter once heard someone at a party ask who wrote the song 'Some Enchanted Evening,' which was being played at that moment. He replied, "Rodgers and Hammerstein, if you can imagine it taking two people to write one song."

At the risk of calling Cole Porter unimaginative, I'd say there are thousands of songwriters who *can* imagine it taking two people to write a song. Anyone who has ever been stuck for a second-verse lyric or a bridge melody has not just imagined, but probably wished for an able collaborator to help him or her through the tough parts.

In Porter's circle of peers – Broadway and Tin Pan Alley writers of the thirties and forties – the majority of songs were collaborations involving two writers, one of whom wrote words exclusively, the other music. That standard lyricist-composer arrangement is only one limited case of what this book is about. It is a case where the lines of responsibility are clearly drawn between words and music. What there is to learn about that type of collaboration amounts to finding a partner whose lyrics or melodies are compatible with yours and whose work habits and goals are compatible with yours – no simple tasks, granted, but relatively clearcut nevertheless. From that point on, the primary task is simply to be proficient at writing either lyrics or melodies, whichever is your speciality.

That's the way traditional collaboration should work in theory, but in practice, even those clearly drawn lines are often crossed. Richard Rodgers and Oscar Hammerstein II were not above changing their own respective melody or lyric if the other had a better suggestion. Alan Jay Lerner wrote the bridge lyric to 'Thank Heaven for Little Girls,' but he didn't know he had it until many attempts later, when his partner, Frederick Loewe, finally asked him exactly what it was he wanted to say. Similarly, it was composer Harold Arlen who looked through lyricist Johnny Mercer's rough notes for 'Blues in the Night' and discovered there among Mercer's rejects the song's famous first line, 'My mama done tol' me, when I was in kneepants.'

Jack Keller, a melody writer who worked with both Gerry Goffin and Howie Greenfield at Aldon Publishing (the legendary Aldon staff also included Neil Sedaka, Carole King, Barry Mann and Cynthia Weil), goes a step further. "I work with a lyricist in a way that I write the song completely with them," Keller says. "I don't write the rhymes but I work with the lyric content and thought continuation right down to the punch line."

Much of popular songwriting today goes yet another step further, to the point where there is no lyric/melody division of responsibility. Often, neither writer does lyrics or melody exclusively, although many have a preferred area or an area in which they are expected by their co-writers to carry the load. Today, it's by no means unusual for a writer to go into one co-writing session with a near-complete set of lyrics, and the next day go into another session with a title and a melody.

The give and take between writers, the shared creative process, the social dynamics between two or more people, the possibility that the whole (the song) may be totally unrelated to the sum of the parts – all these things combine to make collaboration not just different from writing alone, but also somewhat of a mystery to the uninitiated.

It certainly was a mystery to me. My first exposure to co-writing came at the same time as my first efforts at songwriting, in my mid-teens. I was writing alone, but two members of the band I was in wrote together regularly. I think their primary reason for collaborating was the fact that John Lennon and Paul McCartney did (at least, it appeared from the writing credits on Beatles songs that they did), and my bandmates fully intended to be the next Lennon and McCartney. I, on the other hand, intended to be the next Bob Dylan, and later, the next Jim Webb, so I went one better than Cole Porter. Not only could I not imagine *why* it took two people to write one song, I could not imagine *how* they did it.

I can't teach you exactly how to co-write a song any more than I can teach you how to be creative. Even if I could, the same method wouldn't apply to every song and every writer. What I *can* tell you is some things about working with one or more writers on a song. I can tell you about some of the pleasant aspects to anticipate and pitfalls to avoid, along with some real-life writing situations – in short, some knowledge that should make your songwriting more enjoyable and productive.

Since I'm not going to attempt to teach you to write, I'm assuming you have already written some songs or partial songs. More importantly, I'm assuming you write for reasons other than pure personal gratification or therapy. In other words, you want to be a professional, you want your songs to be performed publicly, and you hope to make some money from them.

And since you want to be a professional, I'm assuming you want to be recognised as such by your peers as well as by the general public. Professional-level writing is one element of that recognition; a professional attitude is just as important. Writing as a profession is similar in that way to any other profession. There are certain responsibilities and courtesies that your partner or partners can reasonably expect of you, such as showing up on time for appointments, showing up ready to work, and generally doing what you say you'll do.

The rules set down in this book are not carved in stone, but they are based on common sense. It doesn't make much sense, for example, to pitch 'If Drinking Don't Kill Me (Her Memory Will)' to a gospel artist like Amy Grant. I suppose, though, that anything is possible, and that there could in the future be some circumstances so bizarre that such a pitch would not be inappropriate. In a more realistic scenario, if you're a lyricist, it doesn't make much sense to collaborate with another lyricist. Still, there might be some exceptional circumstance under which such an unlikely team could be productive.

When it comes to interpreting these rules, a lot of grey areas evolve. A simple, straightforward rule like 'Show up ready to work,' for example, means 'Show up sober' to most people, but plenty of hit songs were written in a variety of abnormal mental states, both natural and artificially induced. Thus, the meaning of 'ready to work' can vary depending on the particular writer and the particular time.

One philosophical point that I've already touched on and will continue to stress is the belief that experience is the best teacher. You wouldn't try to learn how to play the guitar by reading a book: you would learn by playing, with the book as a guide. Collaboration is no different. The information and advice contained in these pages will be of little use to you if you don't try actually writing with someone.

I'm assuming that since you've already made some attempts at songwriting, you know the very basic terms of the craft, such as *lyric, melody, chords, changes, modulation, line, verse, hook, chorus, bridge,* etc. If you don't, you should. It would hardly be professional to ask someone to write a song with you when you don't even know what a song is. For instance, if someone talks about resolving the D/E to the A they shouldn't lose you. That's basic songwriting lingo and a part of the craft side of the business. Don't be fooled by the self-effacing type who looks down at his feet and says "Man, I just happened to be there holding the pen when that song wrote itself." No matter how uneducated the guy is, unless he's a one-hit fluke, he knows something about the craft of songwriting. He may not ever use a D chord over an E bass, but he knows what it is.

Even if you do know what a song is, you may not be familiar with the workings of the music business or some of the common terms used in this book.

As for the business, you need to have some understanding of the steps between writing a song and cashing the royalty cheque. There are several books on the market that explain the business in detail. Here is the briefest of explanations. The *songwriter* writes a song. As the writer, he is entitled to *publishing royalties.* He will probably assign his publishing rights to a *publisher,* in return for a percentage of those royalties. The publisher tries to get a song recorded by an *artist.* The publisher may play it for an artist or for the artist's *producer,* the person who oversees the recording sessions. Once a song is recorded and released, the record company may have *promotion* people, or *pluggers,* call radio stations to encourage airplay. *Performance royalties* (primarily from radio airplay) are collected by PRS, the organisation that licenses performance rights; they are then paid either directly to the writer, or to the writer's publisher, who takes his cut and passes on the balance to the writer. *Mechanical royalties* (from record sales) can be paid directly by the record company to the writer or publisher; often, though, they are collected in the first instance by MCPS – the organisation concerned with mechanical rights.

Some terms you'll see on the following pages are part of the everyday music business vernacular. A *cut* is a recording. A *cover* is also a recording, but usually an additional recording after the original. A *copyright* (in addition to the legal sense) is a song in general and often a much-covered, money-making song. A *pitch* is an attempt to get someone to record a song. A *demo* is a demonstration recording that will be pitched to an artist or producer or A&R person. A *master* is a recording intended to be released as a record. A *plugger* pitches demos. A *catalogue* is all the songs you have written or all the songs in a publishing company. A *hold* is a notification of intent to record by an artist or producer, and along with it, a request not to pitch that song to anyone else. A *retainer* is an amount a publisher regularly advances to the writer against future royalties. A *staff writer* has agreed to write exclusively for one publishing company, usually in exchange for a *retainer*. *A&R* stands for *Artists and Repertoire,* and refers to the department of a record company responsible for finding songs and producing artists. *R&B* stands for *rhythm & blues,* and refers to black music in general and often more specifically to soul music. A *trade paper* is one that contains record charts and other news of the music business.

And while we're on the subject of terms, the term *collaboration* to me still carries the old-time connotation of a composer and a lyricist, while the more popular term *co-writing* means simply more than one person writing a song. However, since those words may have different shades of meaning to different people, in this book, *collaborator, co-writer* and *partner* all mean 'someone you write with,' and they will be used interchangeably.

You'll notice that very few of the songwriters mentioned in the text are identified by their works or their partners. I did not want to shut down every thought in mid-sentence with what would be either an incomplete or a redundant explanation of who a writer is, so I've listed all the writers who are *not* identified in the text in a separate Appendix, along with a few of their best-known works and the appropriate co-writers. If a writer is not listed, check under his co-writer's listing.

I am aware that many songwriters, publishers, artists and other music-business people are women, despite the fact that I almost always refer to them as *he*. So wherever I have written *he*, I really mean *he or she*.

At some point in any co-writing session, you'll find it's time to stop chatting and get down to business. In the case of this book, that time is now.

CHAPTER ONE

DECIDING TO COLLABORATE

In the history of popular songwriting in this century, a few names stand alone. Among the Broadway/Tin Pan Alley writers, George M. Cohan, Irving Berlin, Cole Porter and (in the later stage of his career) Frank Loesser come to mind. In pop and rock music, Paul Simon, Jim Webb, Chuck Berry, Bruce Springsteen and Bob Dylan have done quite well without collaborators. In black music, Allen Toussaint wrote many memorable songs by himself. In country, Tom T. Hall and Roger Miller have large catalogues of hits all written alone.

But for every Cole Porter, there is a Rodgers and Hammerstein or a Lerner and Loewe. In every style, there are writing *teams* just as well-known and successful as individual writers – Lennon and McCartney, Lieber and Stoller, Ashford and Simpson, Holland-Dozier-Holland, Morgan and Fleming, Foster and Rice, to name but a few.

For many writers, the initial question of collaboration is not *how* but *why*. For someone like Dennis Morgan, the answer was easy: "I came to Nashville writing by myself, wrote a lot of songs by myself, and didn't have a damn bit of success by myself." It was an easy decision for Roger Greenaway, too. He had had a bit of success writing alone but, he explained, "I hate writing by myself. I don't like doing anything by myself, really. I'm always happier when I have one other person or a few other people around. I'm a gregarious person. I like to share things."

On the other hand, some writers don't feel there's anything to gain by collaborating. Tom T. Hall likens it to having a garden and then hiring a gardener. He has no interest in what he feels is the reconstruction of someone else's thoughts, and he calls co-writing "a lazy man's way of writing."

I'm not here to argue with Hall or any other *successful* lone songwriter. The old saying "You can't argue with success" has never been truer – with one small qualification. If you are successful writing by yourself, and more importantly, *completely satisfied* with your work, then you have no need for either a collaborator or this book. But if you want to explore ways to improve some or all facets of your work – and consequently your income – read on.

Collaboration is a far more complicated issue than, as Cole Porter questioned, whether or not it takes two people to write one song. Dave Loggins wrote 'Please Come to Boston' by himself and Don Schlitz wrote 'The Gambler' by himself. Both of these writers obviously know how to write a song by themselves, yet they chose to collaborate, and among their results are the country hits 'I Love Only You' and (with Lisa Silver) 'Forty Hour Week.' So there must be something more to it than the ability to write a whole song.

Some writers absolutely *need* a partner, some only *prefer* working with a partner, and some may want or need a partner depending on their mood or the particular song they want to write. For whatever reason, most hit songwriters believe there is something to be gained by collaboration (to prove this point take a look at the charts).

Some aspects of collaboration are obvious. A person who writes only music, for example, would benefit from working with a lyricist. On the minus side, the writer of half a song makes only half as much money as the writer of a whole song. But there are many more subtle aspects to consider in deciding whether or not to co-write.

First the advantages.

Complement Deficiences

If you are particularly strong with music and weak with lyrics, or vice versa, you could benefit from a collaborator whose strength lies in the areas where you are weak. When Paul Williams first began to write songs, his confidence as a melody writer was undermined by his lack of musical training and by the empirical evidence that his music was, in his words, "really boring." He actively sought collaborators, and he ended up with an extra unexpected dividend from working with them. They not only complemented his deficiencies, they also helped correct those deficiencies, to the point that he now credits his co-writers with his musical education.

That's an obvious case, a lyricist in need of a composer. It illustrates the classic Broadway/Tin Pan Alley reason for collaborating, a line of reason based on the belief that no one can be good at both lyrics and melodies. But it's not always a matter of being good or not. For Richard Kerr, it's a matter of interest. He does write his own lyrics, but they turn out to be 'dummy' lyrics 99 percent of the time. As he explains it, he is "really into melodies" to the point that he just doesn't want to spend the extra time it would take him to perfect his lyrics.

Other kinds of strengths and weaknesses don't fall into the lyric/melody categories. For example, it is likely that at some time you will come up with a chorus or a first verse that is complete both melodically and lyrically, but then you get stuck. You need a new direction, and you seem to be locked into a train of thought that leads nowhere. Or maybe you have several possible directions and can't decide which would be the most effective. I wouldn't necessarily characterise this situation as a weakness or deficiency (you could call it a tendency not to finish songs), but it is a common problem that a second writer might help solve. This was, in fact, the working arrangement that produced many of The Beatles' hits. According to John Lennon, he and Paul McCartney seldom wrote "eyeball to eyeball"; one usually started a song alone and called in the other to provide a *middle eight* (bridge) or finish up in some other way. (Lennon later amended his statement and admitted that many tunes, particularly the early ones, *were* written together.)

Another scenario. Your songs are full of unique, brilliant lyrical and melodic phrases, but they don't always belong in the same song with each other. You've got the creativity, but you could use some craftsmanship. An experienced collaborator could not only improve your songs (and thus your chances of getting them cut) he could also indirectly fill a sort of mentor role, helping you improve your own craftsmanship.

Increase Your Output

Irving Berlin knocked out five songs for *Annie Get Your Gun* over a weekend. A frantic publisher pleaded with Dallas Frazier one afternoon to get busy on some songs for the demo session scheduled the next morning, and Frazier responded with six tunes, among them the George Jones hit 'If My Heart Had Windows.' Don Gibson wrote 'I Can't Stop Loving You' one afternoon, and then, before he could put his pen down, wrote 'Oh Lonesome Me.' Don Schlitz wrote in 20 minutes all but the last verse of 'The Gambler' – one of three songs he wrote in a two-hour flood of creativity he describes as nearly automatic writing.

Almost every professional writer has a story about an amazing writing binge. But that's just what it is – a binge, an occasional (if you're lucky) happening. Hardly anyone can keep up that kind of pace with any consistency of quality.

A more common scenario for the writer working alone is Kris Kristofferson's writing of 'Me and Bobby McGee,' in which many months went by from the time Fred Foster (his publisher) gave him the idea to the time Kristofferson actually completed the song. Jimmy Webb told Johnny Carson he wrote 'Up, Up and Away' in about half an hour, but that he had had it in his head for years. Dallas Frazier, when questioned about the incident related above (which he did not specifically remember), said he often wrote the songs down that quickly, but that he had been thinking about them for weeks.

Some songs do seem to write themselves in a matter of minutes, but with others you may find yourself spending a great deal more time – a day, a month, a year or more – thinking about it, letting it rest or ferment, pulling it out and reworking, fine tuning. In most cases, the writing process can be speeded up at every turn with a collaborator, for the simple reason that two people will come up with twice as many ideas as one. Consequently, while you may still have 'dry periods' – times when you can't come up with song ideas – those periods can still be productive if someone else is furnishing the ideas.

Bob Morrison is the type of writer who likes to have ideas going all the time, 'to have some wood in the fireplace,' as he puts it. But he has found that the more successful he has become, the more time he's had to devote to business and the less he's been able to spend being creative. Consequently, he freely admits that he sometimes has no ideas. And in those times when his 'wood' supply gets low, he relies on his collaborators for ideas.

Nickolas Ashford has said there are times when he feels creative and his wife and writing partner Valerie Simpson does not, but as Simpson explained, "If there's a really strong creative pull from either one of us, it will pull the other one. Like if I'm really on to something, I can pull him with me because the vibes are so strong I'm just bursting."

Getting unstuck is easier, too, with a partner. Again, Valerie Simpson explains, "With the two of us writing together, it's very seldom we'll both get blocked at the same time. If I'm stumped musically and Nick is really up on an idea lyrically, his enthusiasm is enough to unblock me."

With the second opinion, the fresh viewpoint, and the extra input provided by a writing partner, you'll probably find that you get more work done before you decide to call it a day.

To Dennis Morgan, this productivity factor, when viewed in the context of his career goals, was a strong enough force to make him overcome his anxiety about co-writing. "I realised, because I wanted to write every day of my life, that for me it was going to be a better route to find collaborators and learn how to work with people. I was really shy in those days. It was hard, very hard."

An additional factor, as pointed out by Dave Loggins: "Writers who are prolific quite likely have more ideas than they can personally finish." In Loggins's regular co-writing situation (described in detail in Chapter 8), he will often start an idea with one co-writer while he is still finishing a song with another writer. "It's like food," he said. "Let's feed off each other." The resultant increase in productivity made him, by his estimate, 10 times as prolific – and, significantly, with no decrease in quality. "J. D. Martin and I wrote four songs in one week one time and three of them were hits. Writing four songs a week is impossible for me. I don't think I can do it."

Do you really need to write a lot of songs? No, you could write just one song a year *if* that song is a great song and you get it cut quickly and the record company thinks the cut is so great (by now it's out of your hands) that they release it as a single and the single goes Top 10. If that happens every time you write a song, you could do all right on one song a year. You could impress people at parties and even have a clear conscience when you tell them you are a professional songwriter. Just as long as you don't have an off year.

You can try it that way, but the odds of getting your songs recorded will increase if you have more songs to pitch. One song, no matter how great, is not going to be right for every artist. And ideally, you want something in your catalogue that you could pitch to every artist.

Also, if you're paying attention to your writing, you are probably learning with every song. Through collaboration, you could speed up that learning process as well as build your catalogue.

Get Instant Feedback

If you're on the wrong track, you won't have to labour through the song, put it down on tape, get a publisher on the phone, make an appointment or leave the tape, and come back later to find out you're on the wrong track. Your co-writer will let you know right away. This ever-ready second opinion will probably add to the quality of your work, and because of the time savings, to the quantity, too.

Widen Your Range

Few writers can write in any style for any type of artist, but most writers – for financial reasons as well as for artistic satisfaction – would like to. Barry Manilow at one point worked with four different lyricists because, he said, "They each contribute different types of lyrics that spur me on to different types of music." His four partners brought romantic, theatrical, contemporary and folk influences to his music.

Dave Loggins, who also works regularly with three or four collaborators, concurs. "My spectrum's very broad," he explained, "from a George Jones waltz to a Dirt Band 2/4 type thing to a rock-and-roll shuffle to Marvin Gaye – I've got it all in me . . . The co-writing thing really helped get out of me each root that was in me in maximum form, from country to rock to r&b. I've done a little bit of all of it with the help of co-writers."

In addition to making the most of your musical roots, collaboration may provide you with a way to take advantage of ideas for which you have no roots, ideas you simply can't write by yourself. Say you're a pop songwriter and you have an idea that is a play on words or that has to do with honky tonks or stock car racing or large women in small jeans, a title like Bob McDill's 'Red Necks, White Socks and Blue Ribbon Beer' or Harlan Sanders and Rick Beresford's 'If Drinkin' Don't Kill Me (Her Memory Will),' an idea that begs – even demands – to be written as a country song. *But,* you're London born and bred and you're not particularly knowledgeable about country music – except to know a good country title when you have one. You have several alternatives. You can write what you *think* is a country song, running the risk of placing armadillos in Tennessee or populating Kentucky with Cajuns or, God forbid, using a diminished chord. You can do some research – listen to some country records and hang out at what might pass for a honky tonk in Tunbridge Wells – activities that will be time consuming and will not necessarily lessen the risks of the first alternative. You can call up your regular writing partners, who don't know any more about country than you do. Or you can call a writer who does know how to write country and suggest a collaboration. If you want to get your song cut, the last option is the only one that makes sense.

You don't have to be a country writer to write a country song, or a pop writer to write a pop song, if 1) you know the basic craft of songwriting and 2) your co-writer knows how to write in the desired style. This aspect of collaboration is particularly interesting because it is one case in which a songwriter's limitations – such as being able to write only country or only blues – are really an asset, an area of specialisation.

There is also the possibility that you will widen the range of your writing, because for some unknown reason, the songs you write with a certain partner are unlike anything either of you writes alone. In other words, the total is different from (and ideally greater than) the sum of the parts. Think of the ironic combination of sodium and chlorine, two dangerous elements, which makes salt, an essential to life. The chemistry between two songwriters can be just as unpredictable.

Increase Your Exposure

If you increase the volume of your work and increase the variety, you can hardly help but increase your exposure by working with collaborators – assuming, as always, that you, your partners and your publishers are actively trying to get your songs cut. Any time a co-writer pitches a song, your name goes with it. Whether you are pitching to producers and artists or trying to interest a publisher, the efforts of your co-writers will help to get your name around town. The more people who have heard your name, the better – even if you don't have any cuts yet, even if they don't know exactly why your name rings a bell.

A common observation, usually made after a song has been rejected, is: "If this tape had said 'By Troy Seals' on it [or John Bettis or Tom Snow or any writer with some hits], they would have cut it in a minute." There's a grain of truth there. In a chancy business like music, it's human nature to go with a winner, and in a hypothetical situation where all other considerations are equal (which, of course, they never are), a song from a proven writer will get the nod over one from an unknown. Any producer with a sense of pride will argue the point, claiming that he bends over backwards to make sure he picks the best songs for his artist, regardless of who the writers are. Nevertheless, there is more to getting a song cut than writing a good song, and you've got a better chance of getting someone on the phone, getting an appointment, getting a song heard – all the activities that can influence the supposedly purely creative decision of whether or not to cut a song – if the person whose attention you seek already knows who you are.

Even if you write with only one partner and the two of you are virtually inseparable, attacking the music industry as a single entity, that entity is nevertheless made up of two individuals whose circles of acquaintances must at some point diverge. Someone somewhere is going to know your name because he knows your partner, not because he's met you personally. The more the better.

Advance Your Reputation

Reputations may not get songs cut, but they definitely get songs heard. You can advance your own reputation by writing with people who are better known than you are. While that may seem to be an ego-motivated pursuit, look at it this way: Would you rather approach a producer with "I'd like you to hear a song I wrote with Barry Mann" or "I'd like you to hear a song I wrote with my brother-in-law, a school teacher in Burnley?"

The music business is like any other business in one respect: merit is only one of many factors involved in achieving success. If you can open a door by dropping a name, you'd be a fool not to. You cannot count on a good song getting cut just because it's a good song. You may have to lobby for the song, to convince someone that it is good. A successful songwriter's name on that song supports your case. And a catalogue of songs written with well-known writers, even if most of those songs are as yet uncut, indicates that those writers think enough of your abilities to write with you.

Writing with a better-known writer is, unfortunately, no guarantee that your song will turn out better. You may not be compatible, or you may not hit it off on that particular song. Or, for reasons discussed in the next chapter, *better-known* may not mean *better*. But regardless of the song that comes out of it, the association could still prove useful for gaining contacts or merely for the experience.

Increase The Quality of Your Work

As in woodworking or drawing or any other craft, your writing craftsmanship should improve the more you work at it, alone or with a partner. Working with a partner, you have the extra advantage of watching someone else at work. You can hardly help but compare methods and refine your own. If you always write from the top of a song (writing the first line first) to the bottom, you might find it helpful to know how to work from the middle or from the hook line backwards.

If you always need a title to start from, you might find it enlightening to work with someone who always starts with an instrumental riff.

With two writers, the creative and critical resources are doubled. Even if the duties are split cleanly along lyric/melody lines, no lyricist can resist suggesting what he feels is a better melodic idea if his collaborator is stuck, and vice versa. As any creative artist knows, it's difficult to be objective about your own work, and the comments from an objective source can be invaluable. A co-writer splits the difference between the two perspectives. He can be more objective than you can when it comes to your ideas, and you have the assurance that he shares the same concern about the song as you do, since it is his song too. It should be noted that these creative and critical advantages work only when egos are kept in check.

Work Your Way Into a Publishing Company

It's very difficult for a beginning writer to be a successful publisher as well. To oversimplify, one is a creative job while the other is first a sales job and then, after the 'sale' is made, an administrative job. There are two great advantages to associating with a publisher. One, the obvious, is that you have a representative trying to exploit your songwriting talents in many different ways, such as pitching your songs, lining you up with other co-writers, and pitching you as a recording artist (if that's a possibility). The other advantage is financial. The publisher, if he believes in you, will want to sign you to an exclusive contract for which he will advance you some money. It may or may not be enough to cover your living expenses, but the idea is to allow you to spend more time on writing. He will also cover any administration costs and will either pay or advance you your demo costs. (There are also some traps inherent in an exclusive publishing deal, but for this discussion, I'm assuming you want to be a staff writer.)

Unfortunately, it's increasingly hard for a new writer to get in the door of a publishing company, much less get on staff. Once upon a time, you could walk in the door of practically any publishing company with a tape in hand, some of them with just a guitar, and someone would listen to your songs. Later, you had to make an appointment. Still later, you had to leave a tape with the receptionist unless you knew the person you wanted to make an appointment with. Now, some publishing companies are telling writers, "We are not accepting any outside material" (which may sound contradictory to being in the business of finding songs, but which probably means the publisher has his hands full meeting the demands of his staff writers), while others gain some publicity by announcing an open-door policy for new writers, as if it were a revolutionary concept. They have their reasons for shutting the door (one of them being the minuscule percentage of listenable songs that come in that way), but the result is that it's tough on the new writer.

One way of getting in the door is to write with the writers who are already in. A publisher absolutely cannot ignore you if you have written a song with one of his staff writers, because you control your half of the copyright. At some point he must listen to the song and decide whether he wants your half, too. If you are not affiliated, officially or informally, with any publisher, you should give your co-writer's publisher first crack at the song just out of common courtesy. (You may have already made some such arrangement before the writing of the song.) If the song is not too good, he may tell you you're free to shop it to other publishers or to publish it yourself. Even if that's the end of it for that song, you've made a contact, and unless you're a truly bad writer and/or an obnoxious person, you should have an easier time getting that publisher to listen to your next song.

Assuming your writing improves according to plan, your next effort with the publisher's staff writer turns out well and the publisher slides a song contract across the desk for you to sign. You're giving him *all* the rights to your song, in return for which he promises to pay you royalties at the rates specified in the contract. Believe me, you want and you deserve more than a promise for a percentage of your song. You assume that the publisher will make some effort to exploit your song and thus earn his percentage, but he is not contracted to do so. You've invested part of your life in the song, but so far, the publisher's only investment is the paper and ink of the contract. You deserve something for your song, so insist on an advance against royalties. Even if it's a token amount, say a hundred pounds, you want to get the publisher in the habit of paying for the rights to your songs.

What you ultimately want is a staff position with the security of a regular advance and a publisher who regularly pitches your songs. You've accomplished the first step by placing your song with a publisher. The next step is to write another song with your co-writer on the publisher's staff, or with other staff writers, and continue to work your way into a position of favour with the publisher.

Work Your Way Into a Cut

All things being equal, an artist is going to cut a song he wrote before he cuts one you wrote. So it follows that the best way to get a song cut, other than to do it yourself, is to write it with an artist. That's how Whitey Shafer got Lefty Frizzell to cut 'Lucky Arms.' As Shafer said, "I had a verse, a good melody, and a bridge, but I left a verse open. I sang it to ol' Lefty and he came up with the second verse . . . I did that on purpose."

The next best way is to write with the producer. If the charts are any indication, those are just about the *only* ways to get pop and soul songs cut. On average, about a third of current pop and soul singles are written by the artist and/or producer with no other writers. Another third of these singles are co-written with the artist or producer. Less than a quarter, in general, are written by outside writers, and some of these may have some kind of affiliation with the artist or producer.

Unfortunately, this valuable insight into the music business is hardly a well-kept secret. Anyone with a record deal can measure his success as accurately from the number of co-writing invitations he receives as from record sales. Co-writing with a major artist may not be a realistic possibility if you're just starting out as writer yourself, but you may know someone who is about to get a deal or someone you believe will get a deal one day – another writer, a demo singer, a local club act, a relative. The possible gains are worth the possible lost time.

Have More Fun Wracking your brain for days over a couple of lines is no fun. When a co-writing relationship is working, when some or all of these advantages are coming into play, the work is simply more fun. As Dennis Morgan puts it, "There's another way to do this besides sitting in a room alone and killing yourself." Dave Loggins explains, "[Co-writing] helps you avoid the isolation. I mean, it's difficult to discipline oneself, even with the gift of writing, to stay at it for long periods of time."

Collaboration is more fun because it's easier, Loggins adds. "It was *so* easy. I mean it was work, but having another party in the room made it so much easier. You have more energy in the room. And someone to talk to, for God's sake."

Just like in a good marriage, failures are easier to take and success is more exciting when there's someone to share them with.

Now for the bad news – the disadvantages of co-writing. As I will continue to emphasise, partnerships are complicated animals, and sometimes they just don't work out the way they were planned. Ideally, things will turn out even better than hoped for because the whole turns out to be greater than the sum of the parts, but sometimes the best intentions end up in disaster.

What follows are not necessarily disasters, but they are some considerations that make up the downside of collaboration.

Less Money Splitting the work on a song between two or more writers seems like a good idea at the time of the writing. The writing goes easier, and it's more fun, too. But when the cheques start coming in, the difference between the 70 percent writer's share and the 35 percent or less you're getting could be the difference between a new BMW and a used Escort for your second car, between private and State education for your kid, between writing for a living or selling shoes for you. You wonder if maybe you should have (by now you're sure you *could* have) written that song by yourself after all. Maybe so, maybe not.

Other considerations, though, may offset the cut in pay. It may be that the song would never have been cut in the first place without the efforts of the co-writer or the co-writer's publisher.

On a per-song percentage basis, the pay-off from collaboration is obviously less than the pay-off from writing alone. But writers who continue to collaborate have found that in the long run they can make *more* money, whether it's from having more songs cut or better songs cut. Writers seldom voice serious complaints about cutting their partners in on the profits. (Publishers, on the other hand, have been known to tear their hair and claim impending bankruptcy over too many split copyrights.)

Less Individuality That old lover's name you wanted to put in a song means a lot to you because it brings back some vivid memories. It doesn't mean a thing to your partner, however. And that odd line to suggest a little vulnerability you stuck in an otherwise macho lyric seems like just the right touch to set the song apart from every other macho lyric. It describes your feelings perfectly, but it sounds wimpy to your collaborator.

There is certainly a place for individuality in songwriting. James Taylor's 'Fire and Rain' was an extremely personal song about a real experience. The song itself did not make everything clear (it took an article in *Rolling Stone* magazine to do that), yet it was a hit. Paul Simon has suggested a touch of obscurity to make a song personal. But both James Taylor and Paul Simon have built-in outlets for their songs. They have record deals. They can get away with it. You probably can't.

Words and phrases that have a special meaning to you, that may sound good in the context of the song even though their meaning is not clear to anyone but you, are probably not going to make it past your partner. Don't be too disappointed, though. They probably wouldn't have made it past your publisher, either.

A degree of individuality is likely to be sacrificed when two people work together, for the simple reason that they must work on common ground. They have to write about things they both know about or can at least understand. As Joe Melson puts it, "When you co-write, you get detoured. Then you have to leave the house and get back on the road to find your own theme."

Less Creativity, More Formula Writing

Steve Earle, who does co-write quite a few of his songs, went straight to the point when he said, "I think there is a limit to the artistic level when you co-write. I think my strongest and my most personal songs, you couldn't co-write."

A songwriter-friend of Randy Goodrum's once told him he wondered how Goodrum was going to rhyme *closet* in 'Bluer Than Blue.' As it turned out, he never did rhyme anything with *closet*; the rhyming phrase was *like it*, which only rhymed with the last syllable of *closet*. But because of that remark, Goodrum believes that if he had co-written the song, he and his co-writer would have looked for a different word than *closet* to rhyme, and the song wouldn't have been as original.

A song may have to pass by a large number of ears between its creation and the master session – one or more people at your publisher's, one or more people in the record company's A&R department, the producer and finally the artist, any one of whom could hit the 'Stop' button and throw the tape into the 'Pass' basket. The more people who hear a song, the more toward the centre of popular taste – or *their* perception of popular taste – it must be. It must appeal to a wide audience.

With a co-writer, you add yet another listening test. Somewhere along the way, your co-writer may stop you and say, "I like this personally. But what are we going to do with it besides play it at the office Christmas party? Who's going to cut it?"

The people who are going to cut it are people who, for the most part, are not going to take any chances. The majority of this week's records sound like last week's records because producers and record companies naturally tend to continue with whatever has proven successful. You could write a country song in 5/4 time. That alone would qualify it as un-formulaic. But if you want to get it cut, it had better be an undeniably great song, a song whose greatness overwhelms the oddity of its time signature. The tendency, especially when there are two writers and potentially twice the amount of time to waste on an unusual (and consequently unpitchable) song, is to stay in the middle of the road, to stick with the proven formulas that have the widest appeal.

This tendency is the most serious pitfall of co-writing. It can reinforce those songwriters who aim low, who shoot for the charts rather than for posterity, who imitate rather than innovate, who take no chances. Just as the creative resources are doubled with two writers, so are any tendencies to take the easy way out, to settle for mediocrity.

I'm glad to report that it doesn't always happen that way. If your co-writer is in the right mood, an odd chord change or a strange lyric – the kind you thought he'd be sure to reject – might evoke a response like, "Let's leave it in. I'm sick to death of writing to please a publisher's narrow little conception of what a song is." And it could happen that, if you're both in the right mood as you sit down to write, you agree to throw formulas out the window, and develop a song that makes you feel good. If it takes nine verses and three different bridges to do it right, then that's just the way it's going to be.

Less Self-satisfaction Randy Goodrum has said he prefers to write alone because he feels more satisfied when he's through, when he's completed an entire song by himself. Mac Davis says the same thing: "It's a personal satisfaction to say 'I did it and I did it by myself.' Nobody can take that away from me."

It's not uncommon to hear of a writer who normally collaborates calling his collaborations off for a while. It may be for the sake of his ego – he wants to reassure himself that he still has what it takes, that he can still write a song by himself if he wants to. Loggins at one point became so dependent on co-writing that it began to worry him. He took a 'sabbatical' and spent six to eight months writing alone to re-prove his abilities to himself.

Or it may be for the sake of his craft. Morgan tries to write a song a month by himself "because it keeps me on top of myself." He tries to keep both his lyric and melody skills sharp, he says, "so if somebody calls me, I tell them, 'Yeah, I can do either-or.'"

Or it may be for his soul – he's tired of compromising his ideas and feels unfulfilled. He wants his song to express his own feelings in every line, and he's found that no amount of talk will ever convey every facet of his original idea to his co-writer.

Whether it's better or worse, a co-written song is going to be different from the same idea written alone. "I don't know how to put it in words," Loggins said. "Say a love song, it's an expression of one person's total emotion – lyrically and melodically. Whereas in co-writing you have to get some kind of fusion of those emotions. A song may be perfect to me in oneness [as the sole writer], but to be perfect with a co-writer, it may be different."

Another reason for writing alone may simply be that, although the writer can sometimes use some help getting unstuck, he doesn't reciprocate very well. He can't seem to get interested in writing someone else's ideas.

Anyone is going to feel better writing a whole song than half a song – *if* it's just as good a song and *if* the process of writing alone is not too unpleasant or frustrating. Those are two significant *it*s, and if they apply to you, then you're back at the start of this chapter.

Less Fun

You had a great idea for a song. It's still a great idea, one of the best you've ever had, but you tried to write it with a certain co-writer. You've been quite happy with this partner up until now. But now he's ruined your idea. Somehow, even though you were in the same room as it happened, the song seemed to take the wrong direction at every turn. He never seemed to understand what you had in mind, and he was very self-assured in his conception of what the song should be. It's not a bad song as it stands, but it was supposed to be a great song. You don't feel too enthusiastic about even demoing it, much less pitching it. This is no fun.

You set up a co-writing session with a writer who is on a hot streak. He's got three singles on the charts and he's about to sign a record deal. You arrive with a song idea and you're ready to get down to work. He's calling his accountant. As he's talking, you've worked out the chorus and have the key rhymes outlined for a verse. Now he's calling his Mercedes dealer. You've got the verse melody. He's calling some other kinds of dealers. If he were any other writer, you'd be at your local by now, working on your second beer and telling your friends what a jerk this guy is and how you told him so. Instead, you're working on the bridge lyric, telling yourself that if there's any justice then maybe this horror story will somehow have a nice surprise ending, like a Kenny Rogers cut. This is no fun either.

Those are large-scale examples, but there are small-scale frustrations that occur even among regular, compatible partners. Some co-writers are more compatible than others, but there is almost always going to be compromise. A mature attitude and a controlled ego will help minimise frustrations in collaboration. Fortunately, the bad aspects are only possibilities. They don't necessarily apply to every co-writing situation. Once you gain a little experience, they are usually avoidable. Think of collaboration as a road with a lot of nice sights and an occasional pothole. You can see all the sights; you may hit a few potholes at first, but after a while, you'll learn to avoid them.

CHAPTER TWO

TYPES OF RELATIONSHIPS

Get me to a collaborator, I think I heard you say. You're sold. You're ready to jump in with both feet. You've tuned your guitar and stocked your refrigerator. But before you print out your letter of introduction to Michael Jackson, before you invite your brother-in-law over for a beer and a songwriting session, consider that there are as many different kinds of co-writing relationships as there are co-writers. Some may be more beneficial to you than others. Here are some common types of partnerships.

With an Equal It's hard to define exactly what equal standing is. A writer with a hundred cuts is not necessarily in a different class from a writer with 20 cuts. If, however, those 20 cuts are all album cuts, and the hundred-cut writer has 20 chart singles to his credit, then these two writers are not of equal standing, particularly when it comes to recognition. One gets quoted in books like this and one doesn't. But when it comes to writing songs, they are close enough. If there is a line to be drawn to make a professional delineation between writers, that line should probably be drawn at the first cut. The writer with no cuts is like a fighter pilot without his first kill. Regardless of his skill, he is probably not going to be considered of equal standing with – and he probably will not have the self-confidence of – a songwriter who has had a song cut.

Before too much importance is placed on rating writers by their cut lists, keep in mind that success in *writing* a song is based on ability, which is not necessarily measured by a writer's career success. In the writing of a song, standing comes into play mainly in settling disputes. When one writer thinks a song should be up-tempo and his more successful co-writer thinks it should be a ballad, then it's probably going to be a ballad, especially if the more successful writer has achieved his success primarily with ballads.

The reasons for writing with someone of your general standing are the same reasons for which you tend to socialise with your co-workers from the office, or your football team, or members of your tennis club – people who share the same interests and experiences you do. In writing, those interests and experiences are the bases for songs, and consequently you may have an easier time working with someone who is at your same career level. In the previous chapter, you became impatient with the writer who was preoccupied with his Mercedes. On the other side of the coin, he may be less than sympathetic when you must end the session early because your wife was called in to work unexpectedly and couldn't find a babysitter.

When you actually sit down to write with an equal, you may find that you have a hard time settling arguments, since neither is the accepted authority. But that's not necessarily bad. While you may go round and round on whether to say *ain't* or *isn't*, by the time an agreement has been reached, you can feel comfortable that every possible angle has been explored during the course of the persuasion.

You will probably find this equal-partnership arrangement to be the most common working situation, the primary reason being that even marginally successful writers think of themselves as equals – at least in ability – to the most successful, and even successful writers have some self-doubt from time to time. There are, of course, some writers who have never doubted their ability and have the bank accounts to prove it, and there are some who don't have a clue about how to write a song. But once you've proved you can write a good song or two, you are, as some organisations call it, an associate member of the club. And once you have a cut or two, you're a full member.

Another aspect of the equal relationship applies after the song is written. The responsibilities of each writer do not end with the writing (more on this in later chapters), and when the line of responsibility can be drawn down the centre of the partnership it is the clearest, if not the easiest to toe.

With a Better-Known

One advantage of working with a name writer – success by association – has already been discussed, but there are other advantages, as well as some disadvantages.

Usually, *better-known* means *better*. Collaborating with a more experienced writer provides a valuable opportunity to learn first-hand how hit songs are crafted. Cynthia Weil described Barry Mann as her 'mentor' when they first began writing together. Her experience had been mostly in the area of show tunes, and it was Mann who introduced her to commercial pop music. For Dennis Morgan, the teacher was John Schweers. Morgan recalls one of his earliest 'lessons' as a rewriting job Schweers did on a song Morgan had overwritten. Schweers assured him (although Morgan didn't believe him) that Charley Pride would record it. When the prediction was fulfilled, the student paid attention and learned fast.

Learning from a mentor is a much quicker process than the alternative – playing a song for a publisher, having it rejected, and then going home to try to understand, evaluate and utilise a publisher's critical comments in a rewrite or in your next song. And a collaborator's criticisms are not as likely to destroy your self-confidence as a publisher's blunt rejection. It was for that very reason – to learn fast – that when novice lyricist Howard Dietz received a letter from an equally novice composer Arthur Schwartz proposing a collaboration, Dietz suggested that they first work with more experienced collaborators and then get together, which they eventually did quite successfully.

You assume that a songwriter is successful because he is a good writer, but that is sometimes not the case, or at least not the whole story. He could be a good pitchman, a good publisher or a good self-promoter, and only a so-so writer. He could just have a good connection, such as a sister who is an artist. Or he could be good at being in the room while truly good co-writers write the songs. All of these situations may put more of the writing burden on you, but in the long run (except for the last case), the unequal work load may well be balanced out by a greater number of cuts. The problem is finding out ahead of time what you're dealing with.

Unfortunately, you can never know for sure. As in any co-writing situation, the relationship will vary from partner to partner. Even though you've asked around and found out that your prospective co-writer's only contribution to his biggest hit was two lines in the second verse, you cannot necessarily assume that the same thing would happen if you and he got together. Even with the same writer, the working situation varies from song to song.

Not every successful songwriter is willing to co-write with a writer who may still be learning, but they are probably more open than you think. An established writer is not going to accept a point-blank, out-of-the-blue invitation from someone he's never seen or heard before, but if that writer hears some of your work and hears something in it – like fresh melodic ideas or unique ways of expressing lyrical thoughts – that he can develop into a hit, he may be the one to offer the invitation.

With a Newcomer

To continue from the opposite point of view, if you know how to write a song, you may need only someone to provide a fresh idea. In the same way that a writer's limitations, such as being able to write *only* country or *only* dance music, can be considered strengths under the right circumstances, so a writer's lack of experience can be used to an advantage. Writing with a newcomer, you may lose the experienced second opinion of an equally skilled collaborator, but you may gain the fresh ideas and the enthusiasm of someone who has not yet been jaded by all the restrictive *dos* and *don'ts* of the music business. Be aware in this situation that the job of piecing together and polishing the song will probably fall on your more experienced shoulders.

Since you probably know more people in the business than your novice co-writer, you will also probably do more of the pitching. On the other hand, the same naïve enthusiasm that made the song refreshingly different might also carry over into the business of getting the song heard. The novice, not knowing any better, may pitch it to a seemingly unsuitable artist who just might be in the mood for something out of left field. Even if that doesn't happen, if your novice co-writer is dedicated and/or talented, he will soon be an equal with his own set of contacts and connections.

With a Connection

The easiest way to get a song cut is to write it with an artist. The next easiest way is to write with a producer. In those two cases, though, you'll probably have to wait your turn behind some bigger name writers who also know the easiest way to a cut. So go to the next level. Write with a singer who you think is about to get a record deal. Write with the artist's bandleader, or one of his regular session musicians, or his road manager or his lawyer or his mother. What if his lawyer doesn't write songs? Believe me, *everybody* has at least one idea for a song and thus considers himself a potential songwriter.

Here again, you may have to shoulder more of the workload in exchange for the advantages of the association. And depending on whether your co-writer has any clue as to how to write songs, you may sacrifice some quality. You might have been better off writing with a more experienced writer, coming up with a better song, and pitching it through the front door, through normal channels. In that situation, even if it's not cut by the artist you aimed it for, you still have a good song that you can pitch to someone else. But a bad song with a part-time or would-be writer is not just a bad song. It is a dead song and a waste of your time.

With a Clean-up Writer

When you've got a good start on a song but you're stuck for a last verse or a bridge, you need a 'song finisher.' This is what John Lennon meant when he said he or Paul McCartney "helped on the middle eight." Some writers may not have a lot of great ideas but know the craft of songwriting inside and out. Once the framework of a song is laid out before them, they can fill in the blank spots in no time at all.

Some song finishers work so quickly and make it look so easy, you wonder why you didn't just do it yourself. You feel you've just given your co-writer a free ride on a hit idea and it's costing you half the song. But remember, there's a difference between a hit idea and a hit song. It wasn't a hit song when you brought it to him. If it is now that he's worked on it, stop complaining. If it makes you feel better, finish the next one yourself – if you can. But if the relationship is working – if it is producing good songs – then you'll want to continue. And if it's a continuing relationship, your partner will probably return the favour and drop some hit ideas in your lap.

Riff-and-Hook Specialists

The opposite of the clean-up writer is the 'song starter.' The term *riff-and-hook* comes from a comment I overheard Steve Davis make at a club one night. He was saying he had little patience for spending hours pounding away at a song. He was an ideas man, he explained, and if you co-wrote with him, he was good for "riffs and hooks only, man." You got the duty of filling in the rest of the song. (One of his co-writers, Dennis Morgan, revealed that Davis is indeed a great source of riffs and hooks, but he also does follow through and stick with a song until it's finished.)

You can't underestimate the value of song ideas, which is essentially what riffs and hooks are – catchy pieces of music or lyric that a song can be built around. It sounds simplistic to say, but the idea is the most crucial facet of a song, the basis of a song. An idea is one of those things that seems easy when you have one and impossible when you don't. Any writer would rather be stuck somewhere *within* a song than to be stuck *without* a song. One Nashville writer who was dry of ideas asked the bartenders in his regular hangout to pass the word around that he was offering 50 dollars for a good song idea. If you're a capable writer (which he was), 50 dollars for an idea is a steal. Consider Fred Foster's contribution to 'Me and Bobby McGee.' You're looking at it – the title (actually, it was 'McKee'). Kris Kristofferson wrote the rest of the song, but the writer's credit is shared, and that share is worth a lot more than 50 dollars.

If the idea is good, many times the writing will be largely a matter of craftsmanship. Sometimes a title says enough to suggest an outline for the song. This does not mean that if you come up with the title, then your work is done.

Sometimes even with that outline, filling in the blanks to finish the song can be mind-wracking. The guy who comes up with the title and then sits back and watches is going to be the object of some glaring looks before long. I've worked with one co-writer on a song that started as a third writer's title. The third writer was not a professional writer and happened to be working his regular job at the time we decided to write the song. He got a third of it, which he deserved. He had a couple other workable titles, too, but as far as I know they are still only titles. My working co-writer and I were unwilling to continue to do the title man's dirty work for him.

With a Song Doctor

You play a new song for a publisher who thinks the verses are great but the chorus doesn't work. You take it home and rewrite the chorus, maybe more than once, but the publisher is still not knocked off his feet like he wants to be. He suggests you play it for one of the writers on his staff to see if that writer can fix it. If your ego has a problem admitting that you can't write the song, think of it as just a normal loss of perspective from being too close to the song, or as being locked into a certain concept of the song and thus being caught in a creative trap. Your new partner may take the strongest line from a verse and write a completely new chorus around it. He may take one line and use it as a starting point for an entirely new song. You may feel, as Dennis Morgan did when John Schweers rewrote the song that became his first cut, that your original concept has been destroyed. But your ego will survive, and you have a better chance of the publisher's working your song.

Like any doctor, the song doctor will expect to be compensated for his work. He'll take a percentage – up to 50 percent – that you and he will agree on, depending on the extent and effect of his work. This is a vague area, because you can't just count up the number of changed lines and divide by the total (see Chapter 5). One new line or chord change could make all the difference between getting a song cut or shelving it.

There are a few exceptions favourable to the writer when it comes to compensation. For example, it is widely believed that Fred Rose, Hank Williams' publisher, did a great amount of revision and finishing to Williams's songs. Rose's contributions are believed to have been so great that under normal circumstances he would be entitled to co-writer credit, but since he was already Williams's publisher, Rose felt that that was compensation enough – that it was part of his job as publisher to act as a mentor for his writers. Similarly, if Bob Morrison does anything at all to doctor a song, he expects a minimum of 25 percent, if just for his expertise – *except* when he has a publishing interest in the song. Then he believes his expertise is part of his duty as a publisher and that it does not necessarily entitle him to a writer's share. In a related situation, Tom Collins sometimes furnished ideas to his staff-writing team of Dennis Morgan and Rhonda Fleming, but his name doesn't appear on any of those songs as writer. His compensation came from publishing the songs and, in most cases, producing the acts that cut them.

As in the world of medical doctoring, there are some quacks out there. One of them is the producer or artist who wants to rewrite your song – as opposed to first requesting that you rewrite it – and says he won't cut it otherwise. There are varying degrees of legitimacy here. Following are three real-life examples:

1. A producer once proposed that exact deal to me. I probably would have gone along with it except for the fact that I had already agreed to give him publishing on the song – in this case a hefty 50 percent of the total royalty – and did not want to hand over half of what I had left. I stuck to my principles and I still have my 50 percent. Actually, I have 100 percent, but it's 100 percent of nothing. He didn't cut the song and no one else ever did either.
2. A friend of mine, a gospel writer, took a song to a publisher who liked the song but thought it needed one more verse. Without contacting the writer, the publisher wrote the verse, got the song cut by a major artist, and added his own name on the copyright as 50 percent writer. Once again, the publisher already had 50 percent of the total royalty, so it ended up a 75-25 split in favour of the publisher. The writer complained about it and warned all his friends about this particular publisher. But who's to say that the added verse wasn't crucial to getting the song cut? The writer had plenty of legal ground to stand on, since the addition and the split were made without his permission, but he chose to take the money and to work with a more ethical publisher in the future.
3. One way to avoid this kind of problem is to do the rewrite successfully yourself and beat the proposed additional writer to the punch. A co-writer and I had a song that went to a bridge section twice, repeating the same lyric. An artist liked the song and intended to cut it but wanted a different lyric for the second bridge. He didn't actually say he wanted to write it himself, but we thought he might. And we thought he might want some credit for it. Immediately – within an hour – we got together to write the four new lines. The artist liked the first three, so we hammered out a fourth in a matter of minutes. It turned out that the artist *had* written his own fourth line by the time we called (his and ours were almost identical). Whether he was in fact working on more than that one line I don't know, but because we took care of the problem so quickly, the awkward and unwanted possibility of diluting our shares never came up.

Song doctors are not to be confused with artists, producers, managers, etc., who unashamedly demand a percentage of a song, whether publisher's or writer's share, in exchange for cutting it. They are not song doctors. They are greedy sons-of-bitches.

With an Instrument

You don't actually co-write with an instrument, of course, but with someone who plays an instrument – and primarily for that reason. You want to write a song with some jazz changes in it, so you invite a jazz guitarist to collaborate. You want to write a techno-pop song so you call up a synthesiser specialist. Pam Rose and Mary Ann Kennedy, who with Pat Bunch and Todd Cerney wrote the Restless Heart hit 'I'll Still Be Loving You,' admit that one of their motives for writing with Cerney was the keyboard equipment he owned. Dave Loggins, a guitarist, wanted "the input of a fiddle" in a song – nothing more specific than that – so he invited Lisa Silver, a session violinist but a novice songwriter, to co-write. Silver's fiddle music set a certain mood, which gave birth to 'Maggie's Dream,' the Don Williams hit (whose version, ironically, had no fiddle).

A voice is an instrument, too. You probably don't want to write with someone just because he sings well, but according to Dave Loggins (who is himself a great singer), a good voice adds energy to the writing. Two good voices allow you to hear harmony parts as you're writing them, and just make the writing more fun. One note of caution: make sure you don't end up writing a song that only a great voice is capable of singing. It was out of that fear that Frederick Loewe always insisted that Alan Jay Lerner – who was not a great singer – be able to sing their songs.

The obvious drawback to writing with an instrument is that you may have to bear the burden of lyric writing if your co-writer is primarily an instrumentalist. If he is a novice songwriter, you may also have to take responsibility for seeing that the song is properly constructed musically as well as lyrically. Whether that's actually a burden depends on your own level of development. As I've said, there's no underestimating the value of a good idea, whether it's a title or a piece of music or a vocal trick. To a skilled writer, a catchy riff can suggest an entire song almost as easily as a good title.

With Two or More

As any student of basic logic can tell you, when you put two variables together, all the chances are doubled. When you add a third, you don't just triple, you *cube* the possibilities. All the advantages and disadvantages and complications of writing with one partner increase geometrically when a third or a fourth enters the picture. If you don't believe it, think of a story line for a film about two people, and all the possible plot turns that could occur. Now think of a love triangle – three people – and the many, many more possibilities. Three people on a song can add just as many dimensions.

Take a thousand writers and distribute them among the different types of co-writing arrangements discussed in this chapter. Now pick any three. You might have three writers at an equal level of success who can each write both lyrics and music. You may have two whose strength is primarily melody and a third whose accepted responsibility is the lyric. You may have a lyricist, a composer and a mediator. You may have two writers who seem to come up with the initial idea at every step of the writing and a third who applies the polish to the product at the end of the assembly line.

Just because a song has three or more writers credited doesn't mean they all sat down together and wrote it. Two writers could have started it and become stuck for a lyric or a melody or a bridge, then called in the third party – probably a specialist in the needed area – to help. The need for lyric help is one of the most common reasons for calling in a third writer, according to Bob Morrison. The issue is not so much whether he and his original co-writer have the ability to come up with the right lyric, but whether they want to spend the time. "I'd rather get songs out," he explained.

Morrison will call one of several lyric specialists and essentially pitch the song to him, and he will call only when he and his co-writer get stuck. In contrast, Pam Rose and Mary Ann Kennedy's consistent need for a lyricist developed into a permanent three-way relationship with Pat Bunch.

Some other possibilities. Two writers finish the song but are dissatisfied with it and unable to rewrite it to their satisfaction, so they enlist a third writer. A publisher or producer, or someone else along the way between the writer and the record, makes changes that merit credit. The meat of the song is written by one member of a recording group and arranged and embellished later by the other group members, with credit shared among all. Any possibility you can imagine has probably happened at one time or another.

Whatever the arrangement, if each writer is pulling some of the weight, there should be less work for you with two partners as opposed to one. "It's easier," Dennis Morgan says of three-way writing. "I really like it. It's like everybody has their own little designated thing to do but without anybody telling them that that's their part. Somehow it all levels off into a really natural kind of song . . . It doesn't make sense, but it's neat. I find the editing is quicker, too."

Bob Morrison adds, "A writer may not do that much in a room with the other two people, but the fact that he's in the room is like a three-way tennis match, and there's all these minds sparking off of each other. It's great fun, even if you don't get hits out of it, because most of the writers know the whole score, the story, and you get to learn about new people and to react off them. It's neat."

Pam Rose agrees; she offers another reason that three-way writing is easier. "There's just more energy, more feedback," she said. "When you have just two people, one person thinks this and one person thinks that. You're diametrically opposed and you're at a stalemate. Or somebody's in a slump and somebody's not. Whereas with a third, it acts as an energising force."

With a 'Broker' A *broker* is a middleman, a writer who starts a song with an ideas man and then takes it to a third writer, a clean-up man, to finish. The middleman's contributions could include developing the idea, doctoring, refocusing and nurturing the song along from beginning to end; he may end up putting in more time than either of his two co-writers. Or his contribution to the actual writing could be zilch; he just hired out the start and the finish to two different writers and took a piece of it himself as a sort of brokerage fee. That fee is likely to be an equal share or more, which is substantially higher than, say, a standard stockbroker's fee. The degree of peer respect that the broker/writer gets depends on how his contribution compares to his percentage. And as always, there are the intangible considerations. If this broker seldom carries his weight in the writing, but always gets the song cut, you may find it worthwhile to overlook his shortcomings as a writer.

A final caution in looking for a specific type of co-writer: do not label any writer as strictly a doctor or a clean-up specialist. One writer's clean-up man may be another writer's ideas man. It depends on the individuals and their particular relationships. The only consideration should be whether the relationship works.

CHAPTER THREE

FINDING A
PARTNER

Now that you've decided you want to collaborate and you know all about collaborative relationships, you need a collaborator.

Be selective in hooking up with a writing partner. You'll want to look for someone who seems to be compatible with you in a professional sense, both specifically and generally. Specifically, you and your potential co-writer should be interested in writing the same style of music, the same type of song. If you write techno-pop and your new neighbour writes three-chord country, you've found another writer, but you probably have not found a co-writer. In general, you want someone whose writing philosophy and career goals match your own.

"I have certain values in my work," Will Jennings explained, when asked if there were people he couldn't work with. "Like everybody else, I've written good songs and bad songs and some in-between songs, but I'm really trying to write something great every time I do it. If a situation is too overtly commercial – I guess I don't mind that if the music's good, but if it's something where there's not a soul in the music itself – then it's very hard for me to write it. There have been situations where I have written something just to get it finished. It usually comes out very bad, very flat and uninspired."

John Bettis: "I'd love to say that I look for professionalism, punctuality and neatness, but I don't. There is one thing I do look for. I look for people who won't settle. If I'm working with somebody who says 'that's enough,' I know that relationship is not long for this world."

Dave Loggins echoed Bettis's feelings while adding another quality he looks for in a co-writer. "One of the reasons I never did co-write," he explained, "was that I wanted to write with somebody I felt I could get something from, like draw something from. My own personal demand for perfection is immense, and if I was going to co-write I wanted to be around people who have this gift – people I could learn something from or who could enhance whatever I or they were doing. And maybe I could reciprocate."

By 'learning,' Loggins means more than just improving craftsmanship (although for a new writer, that should be a prime consideration). He's also referring to the creative stimulation he receives from a co-writer who can help him widen the range of his writing or progress to a higher level of writing. If he can still learn something from collaboration, you can, too. So keep that in the front of your mind when you're looking for a partner.

As in other aspects of the songwriting profession, you have to be active, even aggressive, in looking for a co-writer. Before two people collaborate, one of them has to say, "Would you like to collaborate?" Sometimes it's as easy as that; other times it's nearly impossible. But before you can ask a potential co-writer, you have to find one. Here are some places to look.

Ads In Music Publications

Magazines, whether local or national, that cover music and carry wanted ads for musicians are good places to look for a collaborator. Even if they don't carry ads specifically for collaborators, they still may carry opportunities to explore. If you write hard rock music, for example, and are having trouble finding a collaborator, don't wait for an ad that says 'Hard rock co-writer wanted.' Look for one that says 'Hard rock outfit ready for big time, needs bassist,' or better, 'Hard rock keyboard/vocalist looking for group to do *original* material,' and then read between the lines. If there is music, then there has to be somebody writing it. 'Original material' means there's a songwriter associated with the group; a phrase like 'ready for big time' or 'record deal in mind' probably means there is original material involved. Check it out.

Don't bother with ads that say they'll put your lyrics to music or perform some similar service. While there is a somewhat legitimate demand and market for song demo services and custom recording services, there is no future in it for collaborators. Whether the offer is made in good faith or not, whether the melody is good, bad, public domain, plagiarised, used for every lyric that comes in, or whatever, this is a service that preys on gullible non-professionals, or to be more specific, suckers. First of all, no 'collaborator for hire' is going to give you a hit tune for fifty pounds. Secondly, you'd be laughed out of any room with songwriters in it if you admitted to such a thing. And most important, as I can't emphasise enough, if you want to be a songwriter, you have to work at being a songwriter. There may be a few shortcuts, but buying a collaborator isn't one of them. If your lyrics are so bad that you have to pay somebody to work with you, take the hint. Get better or get out.

Wherever Writers Hang Out

Again, where there's music, there will probably be songwriters. Clubs and bars that feature live music, particularly original music, are obvious places to meet potential collaborators. Certain bars and restaurants are also known for attracting a music-business crowd. Even if they don't attract a crowd, certain spots may be known as a favourite hangout of a certain songwriter at certain hours. Producers, publishing company executives and wealthy, briefcase-toting songwriters may "take lunch" at a certain upscale restaurant, while just down the street a group of struggling songwriters is commiserating over a pitcher of beer.

And while we're talking about places where songwriters hang out, don't forget the obvious – the publishing offices. Writers do work there, and they are not always busy writing. Staff songwriters tend to stop by their publishing office to pick up a cheque, see what's going on, read the music papers, kill a little time, get a cup of coffee, sponge a free beer, etc. The door is not necessarily open for outsiders to wander in for a little communion, but if you do develop a friendly, informal relationship with a publisher – one where you can come in the back door – take advantage of it.

Musicians

Many musicians are really songwriters who have to play music rather than write it in order to make a living. And many other musicians, who don't think of themselves as songwriters, nevertheless see the long-term income of a hit song as preferable to the lucrative but one-time payment of session work, and thus want to write as well as play. If you're having trouble finding collaborators through the more obvious approaches, widen your circle and check local music shops or the Musicians Union. A college music department is a good place to look for writing musicians. That's how John Bettis and Richard Carpenter met. If you need a lyricist, try a college English department. If these places don't have a notice board, you can still talk to someone, ask some questions, get some names.

Records

If you like a certain record, particularly if you like it because it's the type of song you want to write, it would be a good idea – and a great career move – if you could collaborate with that writer. That is exactly how Kenny Loggins got together with Michael McDonald. "I felt musical empathy with him," Loggins said. "Musically, I knew him inside and out. I sent a letter to his management and said if he'd like to do some co-writing, I'd like to get together." When they finally did get together, Loggins's intuition proved correct. Their first song together was 'What a Fool Believes,' and on the day they finished that, McDonald played Loggins the bits and pieces that later became Loggins's hit 'This Is It.'

Hit songwriters are approached almost as often as hit recording artists, and they are well-practised in avoiding opportunistic co-writers. So if you should stop Bob Dylan on the street and say, "Hey, let's write a song," don't be surprised if he turns and walks away from you as fast as he can, if he acknowledges your presence at all. Of course, there is the remote possibility that *if* you have a great song idea (a great idea is an absolute must in this situation), and *if* you can hold him long enough for him to hear it, and *if* the idea is so good that the songwriter in him suppresses his revulsion at your assault on his personal privacy, and *if* he agrees to write it with you, and *if* the song turns out right, then you might just get a Bob Dylan cut. That's the longest of long-shots. There is another, more professional way to go about this that could yield some valuable by-products, even if the goal – writing with the writer of a hit – is not immediately achieved.

Let's go back to the start. You hear a song you like and you want to write with that writer. It's simple to find out who wrote a song. Just look at the record label or, if it's a single, the charts in *Music Week*, the music industry's trade paper (which will list the publishers as well as the writers). You may not just be able to look up your favourite songwriter's number in the phone book and give him a call (even an artist of Kenny Loggins's stature took a formal route of enquiry), but you can get the publisher's number, either from the phone book or from some such reference book as the *Music Week Directory*. Start there if you can't get directly to the writer. If you have no track record, play some of your songs for the publisher. Tell him you'd like to collaborate with his writer. It still may not be possible, but the publisher may give you some suggestions or put you with other of his writers who are available and willing to try to co-write with you. And if you do get the opportunity to approach the writer you asked for, don't be surprised if his response is "Do you have a good song idea?" A good song idea is the most attractive co-writing invitation you can offer.

Publishers
Publishers have already been mentioned several times in this section because the majority of collaborations involve a publisher, for the simple reason that the publisher – not the record company or artist – is the funnel into which all the songwriters' products are fed. Publishers are where the songs are.

In addition to pushing songs, publishers also push writers. The theory is: the more songs, the more *hit* songs. And the more combinations of writers, the better the chance that one of those combinations will become Bacharach and David; Mann and Weil; or Holland, Dozier, Holland, to name but a few writing teams who met through publishers. Two of the ways a publisher can push an individual writer are: 1) make critical suggestions in the role of a mentor that will speed a writer's development and output, and 2) simply insist that the writer put more time into writing. Both ways have a point of diminishing returns because a writer can only progress so fast and write so much. A third way to increase production is to suggest, introduce, or set up sessions with different co-writers. An active publisher is likely to be more familiar than his writer with many other songwriters, both on his own staff and with other publishing companies.

For once, the publisher's best interest is essentially the same as the songwriter's. If the collaboration is not working, not producing anything out of the ordinary, the publisher will not keep pushing for it. If it's wasting your time, it's wasting his, too, and he will probably suggest that you think about trying a new co-writer. And, of course, if the collaboration *is* producing hit songs, the publisher will start calling you Son.

Socialise
I've answered a few 'wanted' ads in my life but never landed a job from one. Every bit of paid work I've ever had – from mowing lawns to writing this book – involved a personal contact or recommendation. Most, if not all, of my cuts have come the same way – either from a personal relationship with the producer or artist, or from a tip from a friend. The same thing applies to finding collaborators. It's like meeting new friends. You most often meet new friends through old friends.

The only way to establish personal contact, and then take advantage of it, is to be sociable. Parties and other social occasions can provide great opportunities for meeting potential co-writers. Barry Mann and Cynthia Weil have co-written with many writers through the years, and with the sole exception of Tom Snow, they met these writers through mutual acquaintances. Even their introduction to Snow (who introduced himself) came at a social function.

Unfortunately, these social occasions can be torturous events for those of us who are shy and uncomfortable around strangers, in strange surroundings, or in large crowds. It is not just novice songwriters who feel that way, either. Mann and Weil say they are still basically shy when it comes to meeting new co-writers, despite their reputations. John Bettis advises new writers to be sociable, but he admits that he has a hard time following his own advice. Despite his considerable success, he said he could have helped his career even more had he been less insecure and more aggressive in soliciting co-writers.

If you're not by nature a sociable person, learn to be one when the occasion calls for it. You've probably done it before in other aspects of your life –

introducing yourself and trying to make conversation with someone for a potential romance, for example, or asking a stranger to dance. Look at it as just another professional skill that you need to acquire in order to compete. Look at a social gathering as a business meeting. It's probably in your best business interest to introduce yourself to Dennis Morgan or Dave Loggins or Will Jennings, so overcome your nervousness and do it. If you don't, you'll be kicking yourself the next morning for not taking advantage of the opportunity. If you're not having a good time, leave – but not before you take care of business.

If you are a party lover, you'll still want to keep your professional switch on. Just because you're having a great time doesn't mean that you shouldn't take advantage of any professional contacts you might make.

Collaborators may be found in just about any place people can be found. Bob Morrison met Jim and Bill Zerface, his co-writers on the number-one country single 'Angels, Roses and Rain,' playing basketball. So keep your ears open.

Testing the Waters

Collaboration is a lot like swimming; you're not going to learn much until you get in the water. Granted, there *are* ways to work on either your lyric or melody craftsmanship. As Sammy Cahn has pointed out, if you want to work with a great lyricist, take one of Oscar Hammerstein's lyrics and write a new melody to it. Conversely, any aspiring lyricist can collaborate with Richard Rodgers by writing new words to one of Rodgers's melodies. That is exactly the sort of thing Cynthia Weil did when she was starting out – she wrote new verses to Cole Porter songs. Oscar Hammerstein did it on a challenging professional level, writing new lyrics in a black English idiom to Bizet's original *Carmen* score for the opera *Carmen Jones*.

You can take a set of lyrics and put your own melodies to them, and vice versa, but there is one aspect of collaboration you *cannot* work on alone. You cannot write a line and get an immediate second opinion or an immediate second line. As Bob Morrison puts it, "The wall will not give you a response." The give and take, the tossing of ideas back and forth, the "nip and tuck" as Harold Arlen called it, the intangible forces that make the whole different from the sum of the parts – all the unique aspects of collaboration – you simply cannot practise without actually doing. There is simply no way around the fact that, in the same way you learn to write by writing, you learn to co-write by co-writing.

The pitfalls of first-time co-writing are obvious. You may not be compatible with your co-writer, of course. But the solution is simple: find another. You should have gained some knowledge about collaboration, even from an unproductive effort, and you will probably make a wiser choice of partners the next time.

The worst that could happen is that you waste a great song idea. You must have confidence that there will be other great ideas in the future, but nevertheless, great song ideas don't appear on demand. Ways to deal with this situation will be discussed in the Rewriting chapter. For now, suffice it to say that all is not lost. The situation is salvageable if not reversible. As always, you can learn something from the experience. You shouldn't let one bad experience scare you away from co-writing, any more than you should let one broken heart scare you away from love.

CHAPTER FOUR

PERSONALITIES

The word *compatibility* has appeared often on these pages, and for good reason. It's as important to the success of a collaborative relationship as ability, determination, reputation or any other aspect. It's like a balance scale on which all the positive and negative aspects of a writing relationship are placed.

Unfortunately, compatibility is a lot easier to conceptualise than to determine by simply adding up pluses and minuses. Trying to figure out whether or not you will be compatible with a prospective collaborator is like trying to evaluate the potential for a friendship or a love affair with someone you don't know. You can make a list of qualities – blond hair, grew up in Wales, smokes menthol cigarettes, can and often does strike up a conversation with a total stranger, hates camping and religion, loves football, etc. – and make an educated guess. You can do the same with a songwriter – flowing melodies, banal lyrics, writes mostly ballads, starts at 10.00 a.m. every day and works until 4.00 p.m., carries a briefcase, avoids social functions unless for a specific business reason, uneasy around strangers.

As you can see, your priorities for collaboration are different from the social-and-romantic list. The order of importance should go something like this: writing ability, writing style, writing habits, and at the bottom of the list, personal and physical qualities. You can make an educated guess from such a list, but you still can't know for sure whether a collaboration will work.

Joe Melson's six-year collaboration (ending in 1964) with Roy Orbison produced a catalogue of classic hits. Yet despite his great success as a co-writer, Melson does *not* like to co-write. "Basically I'm a loner," he explained. "It takes a close-knit combination to be good co-writers. Roy and I were close-knit. It's like you say, 'Let's go.' 'Where?' 'To catch a train.' 'Why, man?' 'Well, she left me.' And you write a song, 'Leaving on a Lonely Train.' It's one word after another."

Competition brought Melson and Orbison together when a mutual friend told Orbison, who was singing in Odessa, Texas, that there was a guy 18 miles down the road in Midland who was a better songwriter. They were both cocky young singer/songwriters, alike in many ways. But opposites can work together, too. In the same way opposites attract in magnetism and love, you may discover a compatible, productive co-writing relationship with the most unlikely of people.

The unknown quality is emotion. Success – and especially *continuing* success – in collaboration involves more than meshing together two sets of talent. As in any human relationship, the emotional side of a writing partnership can have a considerable effect on the final product.

Personal Differences

Writing ability and writing style, both professional considerations, were put at the top of the compatibility list, and personal considerations were put at the bottom.

You don't have to read between any lines to interpret this to mean that you don't have to be especially close to your partner personally to have a successful collaboration.

"Songwriting is my business," Jule Styne explained. "When you work, your feelings about the person you work with do not affect the work itself; you just do a good job. In fact, it's better if you don't socialise. Then you can be more openly objective to each other's work."

There are plenty of examples to prove Styne's point. Jay Livingston and Ray Evans are still writing together after almost 50 years, but Livingston says they have very different personalities. They have different sets of friends and do not socialise together much. Their preferred work habits are quite different – Evans rises early; Livingston would rather get up late and work late.

Rodgers and Hart probably would have never had two words to say to each other had not music brought them together. Where Rodgers was a mild-mannered family man, Hart was a bon-vivant homosexual. Their work habits reflected their lifestyles, with Rodgers being a very disciplined writer, Hart avoiding work whenever possible. After their initial meeting at Hart's apartment (at which Hart received the meticulously-dressed Rodgers in a dressing-gown), Rodgers was elated to have found a lyricist, but he later expanded that assessment of Hart, calling him "a career, a partner, a best friend – and a source of permanent irritation." His order of words is telling: *career* comes before *friend*.

Howard Dietz had this explanation for how supposedly incompatible partners can maintain long-term relationships: "After about five hundred lyrics, you get to know the composer. If you can stand him that long, you must like him."

Sometimes, though, personal differences are so great they over-power the relationship, even for someone as business-minded as Jule Styne. While he and Sammy Cahn enjoyed a great deal of success together, they did not enjoy each other, and consequently they terminated their partnership.

John Bettis disagrees, at least to a point, with the idea of the personal relationship being inconsequential. "The person you write with should be someone you really admire," he said in an interview. "Outside of talent, I look for the same things I do in a lover. Are we good together? It doesn't necessarily have to be a fun process, but that helps." But almost in the same breath, Bettis reveals that his priorities are the same as Rodgers's: "The single most important thing is the song itself."

If you truly can't stand to be in the same room with your co-writer, you can minimise tension by working apart or by working as quickly and efficiently as possible when you must get together. Successful partnerships – and success in general – are much too rare to let personal differences intrude.

You don't even have to like your partner professionally to have a successful collaboration. You might detest his schmaltzy melodies or his two-syllable limit on lyrics or his mind-lock on going to the IV chord for the chorus. But since Lee Greenwood or Luther Vandross or Sheena Easton happen to love what you and your partner do, you complain only when you're alone, and you praise those schmaltzy melodies when you accept awards. Until your investment portfolio is so solid that money is no longer your prime motivation for getting your songs cut, you will probably continue to write with the same partner for as long as you get good results.

Collaborative relationships are often compared to marriages, and some literally are: Ashford and Simpson, Felice and Boudleaux Bryant, Goffin and King, Mann and Weil, to name a few.

There are advantages to being so close emotionally, as Weil has related: "We have the greatest writing breaks. Bacharach and David never had it so good." But there are some disadvantages, too, to tying a professional relationship in with a personal one. "At the beginning," Weil explained, "it was difficult to figure out if he was mad at me because I burned the meatloaf or because I wrote a lousy lyric. At the beginning, we were writing constantly; now we're more tuned to the relationship. We really have to be very understanding of each other to make it last. You realise that what you have together transcends what each of you is separately."

Common Interests

A better indicator than personality for predicting your compatibility with a writer would be the interests that you share. Rodgers and Hart are a prime example of how two opposite personalities can meet on common ground – in their case, their reverence for Jerome Kern and their progressive, perfectionist attitudes toward show music – and work together successfully. In a book on popular songwriters in the first half of this century, Alec Wilder wrote of Harold Arlen and Johnny Mercer, "They were not only two men who had been professional singers, but they were profound lovers of jazz. Besides which, and most important, their love of the lonely and sentimental, the witty and the warm and the bittersweet, all part of the ethos of popular music, *tended to make them work together like a single mind* [emphasis added]."

Note that the common interests are not things like scuba diving and stamp collecting, but *professional* common interests. In other words, you'll have a better chance of writing a good rock-and-roll song with someone who likes good rock-and-roll.

Trust

You will be baring your soul to some degree to your co-writer, letting out ideas and feelings that, even though they may be presented in a callous, commercial-minded tone, are nevertheless extremely personal. You may also come up with some ideas or some lines that are so bad as to be embarrassing. You have to be able to trust your partner with this intimate knowledge of your personality and talent.

Some song ideas are inspired by sensitive personal experiences or problems. By the time the song is finished and/or cut, you may have enough distance from it, or it may be changed enough from the original inspiration so that it no longer relates directly. The song is public, but the experiences are still personal. You don't want to open the morning paper to find your partner revealing in an interview that one of your song ideas grew out of an affair you had while your current (though probably not for long) wife was out of town. You don't especially want your peers, who think of you as a nice, well-adjusted, sociable individual, to know that the reason you don't write after 4.00 p.m. is that you need a daily session with your shrink to keep you from screaming in public.

You assume you can hide these things from your co-writer, but you may nevertheless find it necessary to reveal something personal to support your position in the course of writing a song. For example, "I can tell you from experience, you feel less guilty if your wife's out of town than if she's waiting up for you at home." Or, "Rats nibbling on your feet is an alcoholic's dream; believe me, in *this* song the guy dreams of wolves chasing him and he can't run and he knows he's dreaming but he can't wake himself up."

Let me add 'and vice versa' to everything in this section. Your partner must be able to trust you, too. The music business is extremely gossipy, so be careful what you say. You wouldn't want a casual remark to end up damaging a writing relationship any more than you would want it to end a romantic relationship.

Respect

You and your partner trust each other not to make your private life public, among other things. You must also respect each other in your private writing sessions as fellow professionals and as individuals. Vincent Youmans made friends easily but could not get along with a collaborator for any length of time. Although he worked with some of the best – including Otto Harbach, Oscar Hammerstein II and Ira Gershwin – he had no respect for his partners and thus no lasting relationships.

Even if you don't *feel* respect – as in the case of the schmaltzy though successful composer – you must *show* it if you want your collaboration to work. If you can't muster any respect for a man's art, at least respect his success.

An obvious part of showing respect is keeping your ego in check, but what it boils down to is simple common courtesy. If you are dead set on a line or a direction for a song, and you dismiss your co-writer's alternative suggestions without consideration, you're essentially telling him his ideas are useless. If you really are determined not to change your mind, have the courtesy to say so and say why. If you've rewritten your collaborator's melody overnight, don't call him up and say, "I've got a better melody." Say, "I've got a different melody idea. What do you think about it?" There is *never* anything to be gained by unnecessarily hurting someone's feelings.

Not all situations are so easily defined. Often, one writer must shut the other one out for a few minutes to concentrate totally on putting a section of lyric or a melody together. Although the partner may be ignored, it's not out of any disrespect and would not be taken that way by a professional.

Mutual Support

Partnership means you're in this together. The life of a song extends beyond the writing, and within the circle of that one song, from the writers' point of view it really is 'You and me against the world.' If your song gets turned down by every publisher and producer you pitch it to, you should still be able to count on your co-writer's continued support. (This is not to say you should be blind to the possible need for a rewrite.) And generally speaking, the fact that someone *is* co-writing with you, the fact that you are not alone in your quest to write something worthwhile, is an unspoken source of moral support.

It's a rare person who has the right combination of energy, self-confidence, creative talent and business savvy that he never gets discouraged, never doubts himself, and never tires of beating his head against a wall. Just as in the actual writing of a song, you have in your co-writer a sort of relief driver, someone to keep the pace if your confidence should slow for any reason.

Loyalty

The comparison of collaboration to marriage only partly applies when it comes to loyalty. In the same way you expect exclusivity in marriage, when you are giving all your ideas to one writing partner, you expect the same in return. But there is a more pragmatic reason for loyalty, as expressed in the old saying 'Dance with the one who brought you.'

Success is, of course, the bottom line, and in the end it may override any or all other considerations. Most songwriting teams who write only with each other do so because they don't want to tamper with their success. It was for that reason that Dennis Morgan was reluctant to write with anyone but Rhonda Fleming. "To be totally honest, I thought about it, and I know she did, too," Morgan said. "But we were great friends, and it was such a unique, incredible thing going on, I guarded it. There were times when other people would say, 'Hey, let's write.' But any time you find something in this business that's working, God, I think it's precious. It's so risky, when you get something that special going, to invite somebody in like that. We wanted to write until we absolutely knew there had to be some changes made."

Jay Livingston wrote with other partners (among them Sammy Cahn) only when Ray Evans was on an extended vacation or was otherwise unavailable when an assignment came up. "There was a certain loyalty," he said. "I would have liked to write with Johnny Mercer. He would have written with me. He would have written with anybody. The first guy that knocked on his door in the morning, he would write with. But I just didn't want to break up the team. So we would never do it."

Roger Greenaway and Roger Cook worked with other partners, but as Greenaway succinctly stated, "As far as I'm concerned, my partnership is with Roger Cook." So when they did work with other partners, Greenaway and Cook shared credit with each other even if only one of them actually worked on the song.

Why were these writers so loyal? Easy. The team members all felt they had in each other as close to a perfect writing partner as they were going to find, and as I've already said, perfect writing partners are about as plentiful as perfect lovers.

Even when more than one partner is involved, loyalty is still valuable. Many, many collaborative relationships are based on the specific skills of the co-writers as they apply to different types of song ideas. Dave Loggins writes regularly with three or four writers, but he still feels a definite loyalty – to that *group* of writers.

Even in a long-term, one-to-one partnership, you don't necessarily hurt a co-writer's feelings by writing with someone else. Mann and Weil find it helpful to write with others when they feel their writing together has become stale. "There is no professional jealousy," Mann said. "I just say, 'I wish I could have written that' . . . When we write together again, there's a whole lot of energy – a fresh approach."

That approach works for Mann and Weil. They are quite successful together, quite self-confident in their individual abilities, and their relationship is mature enough professionally as well as personally for them to be happy rather than hurt if one writes a hit song with an outside writer.

It may not work for you, however. Say you've been writing regularly with one person and the songs are growing stronger and stronger. Then you get the best song idea you've ever had, but you take it to Michael McDonald, whom you've never written with and whom you just happened to meet last week. Your regular partner is going to be understandably upset at your opportunistic move, and he may soon be your ex-partner. If nothing else, he will expect you to show up at your next writing session with as great an idea as the one you took to McDonald.

Guilt

Every once in a while, you're going to finish writing a song with somebody and be unable to find any lines of your own in the final version. You might find yourself in this predicament when working with a writer like Fred Koller or Jimbeau Hinson, both of whom are capable of writing lyrics as fast as they talk (and who can, when they want to, write melodies too). By the time you've taken a breath, they're already down to the last verse. If you have a conscience, you may feel a twinge of guilt. You may even feel like you don't deserve a full share.

Forget that. The only way not to contribute is not to say or play anything at all. If you press the issue, your co-writer can probably tell you exactly where your comments triggered key thoughts, key parts of the song that might not have happened had you not been there. Even in cases in which you really don't contribute your fair share, don't worry about it. If you and your co-writer write together often, the contributions will even out in the long run. (If they don't, you still won't have to worry about guilt. You will only have to worry about finding a new co-writer.)

Like any other type of emotional relationship, songwriting relationships vary. Some may be stronger and more valuable to you than others, and you may find yourself caught in situations from which there is no escape without someone's feelings getting hurt. The standard guidelines for dealing with life in general – common sense and common courtesy – will go a long way toward avoiding those situations.

CHAPTER FIVE

LEGALITIES

Ideally, writing is a creative, artistic pursuit. Even with commercial success as a goal, business just doesn't have any place in writing. After all, without a good song, all the contractual points, percentage splits, and other legal issues are academic. So concentrate on writing the song; worry about legalities later. You don't want to let business concerns intrude on and possibly sabotage the fragile creative atmosphere of a productive collaboration.

At the same time, you shouldn't use that philosophy as an excuse to pay sloppy attention to business. Too many songwriters have a tendency to do that, and the reasons why are obvious:

First of all, they are writers, not businessmen. The qualities most often associated with writers – emotional, moody, philosophical, tortured, irresponsible, insecure, impulsive – are the opposite of the qualities that make for a good businessman. The idea of standing your ground over one percentage point in a contract negotiation makes you feel like a heartless mercenary. It soils the purity of your art. And if the negotiation gets nasty, you may jeopardise a valuable personal relationship.

Second, as if there needs to be any other reason, writers – especially beginning writers – find it easy to assume that there are industry standards for legal and monetary matters and that things like that somehow take care of themselves. That, coupled with their desperation to get in the door, makes them vulnerable to publishers, managers, producers and even fellow songwriters of less-than-average integrity.

That is why you hear writers complain about getting screwed. Sometimes the writer is over a barrel – in a desperate financial situation – and knows he's getting screwed, but in his judgment, he has no better choice. Those who get screwed as a result of their ignorance have no excuse and only themselves to blame. Remember, you don't want to be just a writer, you want to be a *professional* writer. The more you know about the legal side of your business, the fewer problems you'll encounter. Following are some of the legal issues involved in collaboration:

Writing Credit Two writers sit down together and write a song. Each gets 50 percent. With three writers, each gets a third; with four, each gets a quarter, and so on. That seems simple enough, and you will find that to be the case 90 percent of the time. But what happens if:

1. One writer does most of the work and wants 60 percent or 75 percent?
2. One writer finishes up a song that was already 75 percent complete?
3. Two writers complete a song, then one of them – without telling the other –

calls in a third writer to rewrite it, and the first writer is informed that his share is now cut to 33⅓ percent?

4. Same as Case 3, except the third writer is the one in the dark – he thinks he will have 50 percent and doesn't find out until he finishes that he only has 33⅓ percent?

5. A song finisher writes virtually all the lyrics to a song that already has three writers on it, and thus only 25 percent of the credit is offered for what amounted to 50 percent of the work?

6. A person unknown to you rewrites your song substantially, it gets recorded in the rewritten version, and the unsolicited collaborator then demands a percentage for his contribution?

Case 1. When one writer does more work than the other(s), the 'in the room' principle usually applies. That means that anyone in the room when the song was being written gets equal credit. Counting up lines to determine who contributed the most is not a valid way of settling this issue because the final lines may be only the last in an evolving series of revisions to which all writers contributed in some way or another. One writer may have had every single one of his ideas ultimately rejected, yet those ideas may have served as catalysts without which the final version would have never been written. Unless one writer sits completely silent and motionless through an entire writing session, there is no way to accurately assess his contributions. Niggling over 10 percent will get you more enemies than it will good songs. Plus, legally, everyone is entitled to an equal share (as long as there is no agreement otherwise).

If you're the one who has made the greater contribution, this is not as unfair as it may seem. If it involves a regular partner, you'll probably find that the contributions balance out over the long run. Lennon and McCartney found this to be true, to the point that Lennon shared 50 percent of 'Yesterday,' to which he didn't contribute a single note or word, and McCartney did the same with 'Strawberry Fields.' Pat Bunch, who does most of the lyric work in a team with Pam Rose and Mary Ann Kennedy, concurs. "If you took our songs clear back to the beginning," she said, "I'll bet if you tried to divide them, they'd just come out thirds." As we discussed earlier, more considerations than just writing ability go into collaboration, and (as Rose, Kennedy and Bunch will explain later) the contributions to a song are not limited to lyric and melody writing.

If you're the one who made the smaller contribution, and your partner demands, say, 75 percent of the song, then you do not have a clear-cut decision. Legally, 50 percent of the song is yours. Nevertheless, you may feel that the success of the song and the future of the relationship will be jeopardised if you fight for a 50 percent share. The truth of the matter is, unfortunately, that the relationship is probably already doomed if one partner is counting up lines. Do whatever you think is best in this situation. Actually, it probably won't happen very often. Among professionals, if the contributions really are unequal, the more likely scenario would be for the smaller contributor to offer to take a smaller percentage rather than for the larger contributor to make a demand.

Case 2. When a writer finishes or rewrites a song that is already mostly complete, the finisher's percentage may be negotiable up to an equal share. An idea is not *legally* protectable, but by convention, the original writer is the judge of the percentage. It's simply a matter of common courtesy to let the original writer make the offer rather than for the finisher to open negotiations with a demand for a certain percentage. Most professional writers are willing to give up 50 percent of a song in order to get it finished into a good song. (Most have, at some point, *received* 50 percent when they may not have deserved it.) If an agreement on percentages can't be reached, I suppose each could try to take back his own ideas, but that's asking for trouble when the next finisher is called in and he happens to come up with the same idea as the rejected co-writer.

If you have a song that is done, except for, say, a second verse, and you think that would be worth 25 percent, then state it that way when you approach another writer – before he starts working on it. Ask him if he wants a shot at it – second verse only, subject to your approval – for 25 percent. Otherwise, be prepared to give up to an equal share, because once again, counting up lines is simply not an accurate measure of contribution. A couple of words or notes – 10 percent of the song content – could be the difference between a cut and another song on the shelf.

Bob Morrison, who does quite a bit of song doctoring, agrees. "If somebody makes it 10 percent better, if you had to spend 50 percent to get it that much better, you're much better with that, believe me, because it's the silly millimeter longer that gets the song cut."

It's important to note that Morrison does *not* usually take 50 percent. For his changes on 'Looking for Love' he took 25 percent, and he believes both he and the writers who sent the song to him got a good deal. "I usually say, if I open the letter it's going to be 25 percent – *if* I do anything," he explained. "I feel like expertise is worth at least 25 percent, and if you actually do a bunch of stuff, it might end up 33⅓ percent, or whatever. There's usually a bunch of other writers, and it's really hard for me to take over 33⅓ percent because I think somebody will always feel ill-used, even if I wrote half the song. But I don't count words. I don't count melodic notes. I figure the idea's worth 33⅓ percent or 25 percent, depending on how good the idea is. The melody and the lyric are worth an equal amount of whatever's left. It should be an easier relationship than, 'Well, I'm taking 41⅔ percent.' It gets to be a book-keeping nightmare, and you create a lot of ill feelings. It's better just to go ahead and split it some nice, easy, able-to-deal-with way instead of splitting hairs."

It's not always a case of the experienced song doctor cutting into the novice songwriter's work. Roger Greenaway and Roger Cook had their 50 percent interests in a song called 'True Love and Apple Pie' cut down to 25 percent each when they had to share credit with two writers who wrote a new set of lyrics. Greenaway said he and Cook didn't mind a bit. In its original form, the song had sparked no interest, but with its new lyric and the accompanying TV ad campaign,'I'd Like to Teach the World to Sing' made a lot of money for everyone involved.

Cases 3 and 4. These cases are complicated by a misunderstanding caused by an irresponsible writer. Legally, the original contributor in Case 3 is entitled to his original 50 percent no matter how many more co-writers his irresponsible partner brings in; his share can be reduced only with his consent. Legalities aside, as a matter of common courtesy you should *ask* rather than *tell* your co-writer if you want to take the song to a third writer, and you shouldn't do it if he doesn't agree. And, of course, you should inform the third writer that he *is* in fact the third writer on the song and not the second.

If the song is *not* complete when the third writer arrives, then the *intent* of the writers becomes an issue, and the legal situation – which involves proving what someone was thinking – gets cloudy. At this point, you'll probably be better served by advice than by further explanation. That advice is: don't do anything to a song – finished or unfinished – that would threaten your co-writer's interest unless you have your co-writer's consent.

What if you are the wronged party, the one whose share is cut from 50 percent to 33 ⅓ percent? Again, you may have a clear legal case, but you do not have a clear-cut decision. Standing up for your rightful share could damage your writing relationship (which has already been damaged, of course, by your co-writer's actions). But more importantly, once a rewrite is done, two different songs exist. You have to decide whether you want 50 percent of the original or 33 ⅓ percent of the new song. If the new version is more likely to be cut, then it may be a case of choosing between 50 percent of nothing and 33 ⅓ percent of a hit.

As in the case of 'I'd Like to Teach the World to Sing,' a hit record can dissipate any second-guessing over reduced shares. It can even dissipate resentment over an unauthorised reduction of shares, as it did for Alvin 'Red' Tyler. Tyler and Allen Toussaint wrote an album's worth of instrumentals for Toussaint's recording début on RCA, but when the album was released, they discovered upon reading the label on the record that they had gained a third writing partner – the man at RCA who titled the tunes. Tyler bears no resentment toward RCA, however. One of the tunes, 'Java,' later became a pop hit by Al Hirt on RCA, and Tyler says it is the only time in his entire career he has been properly compensated as a song-writer.

Case 5. The actual song this question is based on is 'I'll Still Be Loving You.' Pam Rose, Mary Ann Kennedy and Todd Cerney started the song together, wrote all the music, and then took it to Pat Bunch when they became stuck for lyrics. Unlike the example, Bunch did not demand more than 25 percent. Rather, she was asked by Kennedy if she wanted more than 25 percent. "It surprised me that she would bother to say it," Bunch said, "because she would have known my answer. I said, 'Are you kidding?' How lucky I was to be the person who got to try that. I mean, what would those words have been in a greeting card?"

Case 6. This is 'Hound Dog.' Jerry Lieber and Mike Stoller wrote it and Big Mama Thornton recorded it. Elvis Presley heard it (Lieber and Stoller believe) performed by a lounge singer who sang some different lyrics. That new version is the one Presley recorded. As Lieber and Stoller explained on David Letterman's

TV show in 1987, the new version was an "unauthorised adaptation," and the unknown co-writer neither received nor was entitled to receive the first penny.

The lesson to learn from these cases is to avoid misunderstandings, for ethical as well as legal reasons. If there's any question that your percentage might be something other than equal, then voice that question and get it settled before you start writing. You can't count on every song being a hit and mending hurt feelings. The line is so fine between misunderstanding and misrepresentation (a nice word for *lying*), and the potential problems are so great – you risk sacrificing not only your song, but your reputation as well – that you can't afford to be anything less than totally honest with your collaborators.

Joint Works

Under normal co-writing circumstances, you and your partner create a 'joint work'. Unless otherwise agreed, collaborators each have undivided, equal interests in the song. In other words, if two writers wrote it, they each own half of everything. Even if one contributed music exclusively and the other lyrics, under the joint-work concept, the contributions are equal and indivisible. That means that one partner cannot withdraw his own contribution or remove his partner's contribution without his partner's consent, because once the song is finished, the contributions can't be separated – legally, there is no longer such a thing as 'his own contribution.'

Probably the most important ramification of the joint-work concept applies in copyright infringement suits. For 'You're the Reason God Made Oklahoma,' written by Sandy Pinckard and Larry Collins, Pinckard wrote the lyric and then gave it to Collins for music. Collins wrote the music, and before Pinckard ever heard the completed song, demoed it and got it cut. Carrying the credit line 'words and music by,' it became a hit country single for David Frizzell and Shelly West. Boudleaux and Felice Bryant sued on the grounds that the melody infringed on their song 'Rocky Top.'

The credit line, 'words and music by,' is the key here. It indicates that 'You're the Reason God Made Oklahoma' is a joint work. Since both writers have equal and indivisible interests, they also have equal and indivisible legal responsibility. In other words, if a judgment were to go against them, Pinckard would be liable for a part of the song he had absolutely nothing to do with.

The suit was settled out of court, but it affected more than the wallets of Pinckard and Collins. It destroyed their writing relationship. They have written about 15 other songs together that Pinckard said will probably not see the light of day now. And the experience severely damaged Pinckard's individual songwriting career. It was a prime factor in his decision to quit writing country songs and move into a different field – writing and performing in a comedy duo with Richard Bowden.

Collective Works

You can (as Sandy Pinckard does now) credit words to the lyricist and music to the composer, but that arrangement – resulting in what is known as a 'collective work' – has its own set of complications and inequities. If you're the lyricist, then you alone will be paid for a book of your lyrics or a record of someone reciting your lyrics to no music (realistically, the only potential outlets for a lyricist). Conversely, if you're the composer who is separately credited, you make all the money from an instrumental album of your work. And if foreign lyrics are written for your song, only the lyricist has to split his royalty with the foreign collaborator. If separately credited works are used in a film and the music is incorporated into the soundtrack, the lyricist and composer may have separate agreements, the results of which could be anything from unequal payment to one writer's name being twice as large as the other's in the advertisements.

The advantage appears to be with the composer in a separately credited work – he probably stands to make more from an instrumental album of the team's hits or a melody that is used in a film soundtrack than his lyricist partner is going to make from the sale of books. The potential gain, however, may not be as great as the potential damage to a partnership that would result from excluding one partner from certain areas of income.

You may feel you have more legal protection with a separately credited work, but your relationship may not be so protected. While you may not have to stand as a co-defendant in a suit involving your partner's alleged infringement, your writing relationship may be damaged nevertheless, regardless of the outcome of the suit.

If you are strictly a lyricist or a composer and you have a fear of being caught up in somebody else's lawsuit, by all means insist on separate credit. Otherwise, your partnership will probably be on friendlier terms if your songs say 'Words and music by _____ and _____.

Exceptions

You probably noticed the phrases 'unless otherwise agreed' and 'without consent.' You and your collaborator can have unequal percentage splits and generally make any kind of legal arrangement you want – as long as you both agree to it. You can agree to keep music and lyrics separate, and you can even agree to return each to its original contributor if the song has not been cut within a certain amount of time. Just make sure any arrangement out of the ordinary – 'the ordinary' being a joint work divided equally – is in writing. It must be in writing. (If you have an exclusive songwriter's agreement with a publisher, your flexibility in these collaboration agreements may be limited by the terms of your publishing contract.)

Publishing

The writers' shares account for only a proportion of the total royalty on a song; the rest goes to your publisher, assuming you have one. (If you are self-publishing, of course, you collect the entire royalty.) The publisher's percentage varies from contract to contract. Traditionally it was 50 percent, but this is now generally regarded as unreasonably high, particularly in view of the fact that many present-day publishers act primarily as collecting organisations. Anything from 60/40 to 85/15 in the writers' favour is common nowadays, depending on the bargaining power of the songwriters involved. It is also becoming more common for successful songwriters to 'license' rather than 'assign' their copyrights – in other words, to grant the rights in a song for a limited period, rather than to sign away ownership of those rights altogether.

Do not assume even the obvious when it comes to publishing. While most publishers do not object to their writers working with writers from other companies, they *do*, in most exclusive songwriter assignments, retain the right of approval in those situations. Many publishers also retain the right to require a minimum percentage share in a co-written song. One highly successful publisher absolutely refused to split his percentage with anyone, and consequently that publisher's staff writers could co-write with no one but fellow staff writers or independent writers who were willing to sign their songs to that company. This seems rather unreasonable from a writer's point of view (the publisher wanted to avoid complications if and when the company was sold, which it was), and a few exceptions were made when writers insisted on co-writing outside the company (the publisher's percentage alternated in those cases, rather than being split between the two publishers). If you approached a writer from this particular company, you had to know that unless you gave this company your publishing, you risked wasting your entire effort – your song would have been treated as a non-song.

Here's a less tyrannical and more common situation. A publisher is paying five staff writers a set weekly retainer, regardless of the number of songs they turn in. The percentage-total for each writer comes to one song a week. (A writer who writes two songs with a single co-writer has an output of 50 percent x 2 = 1 song; another writer, working with a three-man team that turns out three songs a week has a total of 33⅓ percent x 3 = 1 song.) If all the writing is done within the staff, the publisher gets five songs per week for his cash outlay. If each writer collaborates with writers whose publishing is *not* available, the publisher gets only a fraction of five songs for the same amount of money. (The publisher's demo expenses are also cut in half, and his marketing resources are doubled with a co-publisher, but he won't mention that.) And if each writer collaborates with a non-staff writer who *does* sign over his publishing – but for a price (an advance) – then the publisher gets his five whole songs, but it costs him more than if they were all written by staff writers. So publishers may from time to time encourage their writers to secure publishing from any non-staff collaborators. Your options in a case like that are discussed more fully in Chapter 16, but no matter what, you need to know the situation before you sit down to write.

Here's another scenario. You and your co-writer are not yet established and your song is published through your own separate companies, which at this point are companies in name only (meaning you have no cuts). A producer wants to cut the song and asks who Greenhorn Music and Novice Music (the listed publishers) are. You proudly say, "Those are our companies," and since you are obviously new at this game, the producer takes that to mean "Publishing is open." He asks for a percentage of the publishing. The artist is a major artist, so the offer, unfair as it may be in principle, is worth considering. You and your co-writer would still retain a substantial proportion of the publishing, and your publishing company would be in business. It sounds like a reasonable deal to you, and you say so. But your co-writer, having just read an article warning newcomers against 'sharks' in the music business, adamantly refuses to give up any of his publishing. You can still get the cut by giving the producer his percentage from your share of the publishing alone, but then your co-writer would make considerably more money (as half-writer and half-publisher) than you. You have several options, the most appealing of which is to shoot your co-writer in the kneecap. The option you no longer have, but which you wish now you had taken, was to discuss beforehand with your co-writer what you – the two of you as a team – would do if this situation arose.

Legally, you're stuck. The one thing you *cannot* do is sign a publishing agreement on behalf of your co-writer. No exclusive assignment of copyright rights (which is what a publishing agreement is) can be made without the *signed* consent of all the writers. It doesn't matter what he *said* he would do. Oral agreements don't count. For an assignment of such rights to be legal, it must be in writing.

Is the co-writer dead set on publishing his part through his own company? Is he going to shop for a publisher? Is he willing to give up part or all of his half in return for a cut? Are you? In the case of a new writer working with an established writer, is the new writer going to sign his publishing to a publishing company owned by his partner? You need to know these answers.

Expenses

So far, this discussion has been concerned with splitting up potential *income*. But depending on the generosity of your publisher, you may also have *expenses* to consider, the primary one being a demo session. This expense could amount to nothing if you or your partner has a home studio and you can programme or play all the instruments and sing all the vocals. But if you do have to hire musicians, vocalists and a studio, it could cost you several hundred pounds per song. If you don't have a co-publishing agreement (which you eventually will need if the song is recorded), you are not *legally* responsible for your share of those expenses. But you are *morally* responsible. (Try telling your partner you don't have to reimburse him for demo expenses if you don't want to, and see how long you have a partner.) So give your potential expenses some thought beforehand, and let your partner know what you intend to do.

Contracts

Any good lawyer would advise you for your own protection always to have a collaboration agreement in writing before you write with anyone. I've never seen such an agreement, and I, like every songwriter I know, would take such a request as an insult to my integrity and reputation. But if there is *any* question – any waffling on an equal split or some vague publishing obligation – or if your co-writer has a reputation for not doing what he says he will do, you probably should get something in writing. And you should probably start looking for a new co-writer.

There are, however, some contracts that you must sign if you do anything with a song, and those are publishing contracts, which may also lead to administration and licensing agreements. If you and your co-writer are both staff writers, even if for different publishers, your exclusive writer's contracts will probably already cover the paperwork for you. In any other case, you will have to deal with contracts.

If you and your co-writer sign your song with a publisher, you will sign a single-song contract assigning him the copyright, which includes publishing rights. This is the same contract you would sign if you had written the song alone, but in this case, it will list all writers and their respective percentages. It will also include your advance if you were able to get one.

If you want to keep publishing open on a song in order to negotiate with it at a later time, that is the same as publishing it yourself. You, as co-publisher, will have to have an agreement with your co-publisher. This could be a co-administration agreement, under which you normally agree to split demo costs (sometimes within a stated limit), copyright and other administration fees and expenses. Or it could be a co-publishing-with-exclusive-administration agreement, under which the publishing is split but one company (for an extra percentage) handles all the administration duties. Either agreement will list, of course, the publishers and their respective percentages. Which one you should sign depends on how effective an administrator your co-publisher is and how much patience you have for dealing with the intricacies of publishing.

A complete discussion of contracts for songwriters and publishers and writer/publishers is a separate book. As contracts apply to co-writing situations, your specific concern should be that the percentages are correct. Your general concern should be that the contract is fair. To that end, it would be a good idea to learn to read and understand a contract yourself. (It is not as hard as it looks to decipher the legalese. Like sentences in normal English, contract clauses have subjects and verbs. Identify them and you're well on the way to understanding.) I've caught inequities in songwriter contracts that reputable music-business lawyers missed. And unfortunately, I've been burned – and it was a major, major contract point – as a result of being over-confident in my amateur legal knowledge. So don't hesitate to consult a lawyer, and make sure that lawyer specialises in entertainment law.

This seems like an awful lot to consider when all you really want to do is write a song with somebody. Fortunately, a minute or two of discussion beforehand about demo plans and publishing obligations is usually all it takes to avoid any problems.

CHAPTER SIX

RESPONSIBILITIES

You may not know exactly what your specific writing responsibilities are going to be until you actually get down to work with a collaborator. Whether you end up doing all the words, all the music, some of each or whatever, may depend not just on the particular collaborator but on the particular song. Nevertheless, some general responsibilities in collaboration – things you and your partner can reasonably expect of each other – apply to all relationships. They will probably seem obvious to a conscientious person, but they are quite important.

Be Professional When the writers interviewed for this book talked about being able to co-write with any writer, they quickly qualified that statement to say any *professional* writer. There are many aspects to professionalism, but they all stem from the fact that songwriting is a business – a business with a creative base, true, but a business nevertheless. People do it for a living – that's what *professional* means.

Don Schlitz calls going into his publisher's office to write songs "going to work." As in any job, it's a good idea to show up for work on time and ready to work. Showing up late is an inconsiderate waste of your co-writer's time, and an irate co-writer is probably not going to be a productive one. Some people, of course, consistently run late, and their *regular* writing partners routinely adjust their scheduled starting times accordingly. The partners may even use that extra time to prepare for the session. But that's regular partners. You don't want to risk aborting a potentially productive relationship because you had a couple of errands to run and were an hour late for the first meeting.

Most of the time, 'ready to work' means *not* drunk, stoned, speeding, tripping, hung over or otherwise preoccupied. But as always, there are grey areas. Many co-writing sessions that start out straight and sober don't end that way. Some writers may feel that a limited, controlled amount of outside influence – one beer, maybe, but no more – loosens their thoughts. One of Dallas Frazier's favourite writing techniques was to grab a co-writer and a supply of liquor and retreat to a cabin in the woods. Some writers find that when normal thoughts are short-circuited by a hangover, they come up with strange, unique song ideas. But even if you *are* able to write well under abnormal mental conditions, if you should fail just one time, consider the difference between someone saying, "I wrote with him once and he didn't contribute much" and "I scheduled a writing session with him and he showed up drunk." The first one is excusable, possibly attributable to a lack of compatibility or just an off-day, and maybe it's even to be expected once in a while. The second one is not. And worse, the second one will get around to other writers faster and will stick with you longer, while the first one will be forgotten as soon as you write a good song. If your behaviour is going to fall into one of these grey areas, save it for writers who know you well and who may forgive you.

Know Your Craft

When you ask somebody to write a song with you, it's reasonable for that person to assume that you know how to write a song. You may not be great at it yet, you may still be learning (most of the great writers will admit that they're still learning), but you should have an idea of how songs are put together, what makes them work. There's no clear line between knowing and not knowing. It's not as if you know how to write a song today, but you didn't yesterday. There is, however, a basic level of craftsmanship you should have reached. You should understand the difference between a song that has choruses and a song that has only verses and a bridge – not just to be able to say that one form is ABAB and the other is AABA, but to understand *why* an idea might be written more effectively in one form than the other. You don't have to buy a book or take a correspondence course to study these things; you can pick up a lot by listening to the radio with an analytical ear.

You wouldn't try to build a bridge without first finding out something about bridges. You can't fake your way through any deficiencies in your songwriting craft, either. What you *can* do is embarrass yourself and hinder the work more than help it.

Have Ideas

Everybody runs out of ideas at one time or another. Roger Greenaway talks in Chapter 7 about how that can actually be a good creative situation. Most pros have complete confidence that an idea will come, because they know how to trigger ideas. Still, they'd rather have an idea than not have one. You wouldn't call a business meeting without some plan. Co-writing is no different. Ideas are the plans. They are part of the preparation for a session – particularly a first session. When you ask someone to write with you, it is reasonable for him to assume you have already given some thought to the matter and that you have something productive in mind. You don't want to begin a co-writing relationship with your partner wondering if maybe you're just using him – mining his creativity and not contributing any of your own. Even if the plan, your song idea, doesn't pan out, you have a responsibility to make the effort.

Work Hard

The responsibility to make an effort doesn't stop with the idea, of course. You owe it to your partner to make a conscientious effort to write a good song. Will Jennings states clearly and perfectly his responsibility as a lyricist: ''Try to write a lyric as good as the melody or give them a lyric that will inspire them to write something good.''

A full effort requires concentration, which means you shouldn't have all your home phone calls – from your insurance broker, your mother, your girlfriend, your vet, etc. – forwarded to your co-writer's house. Writing songs is hard enough without unwanted distractions. It's the only business you should have on your mind during a writing session. Some writers don't mind interruptions or have conditioned themselves to ignore distractions, and they mistakenly assume their co-writers are the same way. I once tried to finish a song with a writer at his house. His young children had been a mild distraction in previous writing sessions there, but this time one of them mistook me for a jungle gym. My co-writer, being used to writing with one hand and changing a nappy with the other, took no notice whatsoever. We finished the song and, as it turned out, our co-writing relationship too.

In addition to concentrating on your work, you are expected to give a co-writer your best effort. What that really means is, don't hold back. If you're saving ideas for other co-writers, you're sending your partner of the moment the implicit message that he is not good enough. If you feel like you would be wasting an idea by presenting it to that partner, it's probably time to look for a new partner.

Respect

We talked about respect as one of the emotional aspects of collaboration, but it is more than an emotional aspect. It is your responsibility as a professional to respect your partner as a fellow professional. You won't have a very pleasant or long relationship if you don't.

Your partner will have as many opinions as you have about writing songs. The more opinions you share, the easier the writing will be. But there will be times, even in the smoothest of relationships, when one partner likes a line, a verse, a title or whatever, and the other doesn't. The argument may get heated, but you still must respect and listen to your partner's side, and above all, do not attack his songwriting skills in an effort to get your way. Unlike romantic relationships, you won't find any songwriters with masochist tendencies when it comes to their work. No one likes to be constantly overruled, especially when there are no hard-and-fast rules.

Compromise

Compromise does not have quite the same meaning here as in a legislative debate. The solution to an argument over two different verses is probably *not* half of one and half of the other. I'm not suggesting you compromise your *principles* – if you find yourself doing that, then find yourself another partner. I'm suggesting that you compromise your *ego* for the good of the song. If your partner thinks there is a better line somewhere than the one you just came up with, then there probably is. You'll find that the more professional your partners are, the less ego gets in the way.

Be a Good Parent

Your song is your baby, and as with the human kind of baby, your parental responsibility doesn't end at birth. It starts there. Once the song is written, it's still a long way from being a record. Depending on your publishing situation, a great deal of work may be ahead for you and your co-writer. You will expect your fair share of the rewards, so accept your fair share of whatever work is necessary to find a publisher, demo the song, and get it cut.

CHAPTER SEVEN

SONG IDEAS

It's a good idea to have a good idea, especially when you get together with a collaborator for the first time. It not only helps to break the ice, it also shows that you're taking the partnership seriously, you've already given it some thought, and you're ready to work. (Don't panic if you don't have any ideas. There will be more on generating them later in this chapter.)

Not all good song ideas are good ideas for co-writing. Writing alone, you may be able to make a good commercial song out of references that are obscure, personal or common, but if you expect to get any help from a co-writer, he has to know what you're talking about, what you're planning, and he has to know it from the beginning. Don McLean was inspired to write 'Vincent' (better known by its first line, 'Starry, starry night') by the life of the artist Vincent van Gogh. He wrote it alone, but I believe he would have had a hard time convincing a co-writer to get into an idea about a person who's been dead almost a hundred years and who's fairly obscure to the people who make or buy records.

The same applies to personal ideas. Imagine James Taylor showing up at your house for a co-writing session, unpacking his guitar, flipping through his notepad, and saying, "I've got this idea about my girlfriend – she just committed suicide – and the clincher line of the second verse is about my old band, the Flying Machine, breaking up, and then we call in Jesus for the last verse. All I have so far is a title, 'Fire and Rain'." Your reaction would probably be, "What do fire and rain have to do with any of that? Assuming anyone even cares about a flying machine that is a band, it's going to confuse people. And why don't we just leave Jesus out of this?"

Common words and phrases are all right in the sense that your collaborator will know what they mean, but they need something more – a bit of melody or a total lyric idea that makes the idea unique. What if Paul McCartney called you and said "Let's write a song called 'Yesterday' "? (Actually, his working title was 'Scrambled Eggs.') If you're familiar with the work of Jerome Kern and Otto Harbach, you might say, "There already is a song by that title, Paul baby. Call me when you think of something more catchy and original."

The problem in all three examples is to come up with a song idea that at least one other person – the co-writer – can envision as a song while it is still in idea form. If it takes a finished song for the idea to become clear, it's too late for the co-writer.

It's not as easy as it might appear to determine what is too obscure, personal or common, and what is not. As these examples illustrate, the key is not so much in the idea itself – all three turned out to be quite lucrative ideas – but the presentation. I have used worst-case scenarios to show how to get an idea rejected by a co-writer. All three songs were in fact written entirely by one person (even though John Lennon was credited with McCartney), but a co-writer could conceivably have taken the bait if the presentations had gone like this:

'Vincent': I have an idea about a misunderstood, unappreciated artistic type, a man who ended up in an insane asylum and produced his best-known work there. It's a situation every creative person today can identify and sympathise with. We can use some material from the life of Vincent van Gogh as a framework, but we don't even have to mention his last name.

'Fire and Rain': I've got this idea about a guy who thought he'd already seen everything in the way of hard times and worlds falling in on him, but the one thing he never thought he'd see was his girlfriend committing suicide, which she just has. I've got some real-life experiences to draw on, and if we make them a bit vague, using them to set a mood rather than painting a literal picture, I think we can hook it.

'Yesterday': Listen to my melody, fool, before you say no.

No matter how clever or unique your idea is, and no matter how detailed your presentation, you are essentially pitching it to your partner. And like a song that is pitched, an idea may be rejected by your partner for any imaginable reason, whether it seems valid to you or not. There is only one sure way to avoid rejection, and that is never to come forth with any ideas in the first place. If you choose that option, however, you will also be well on the way to avoiding co-writing altogether. If your partnership is truly professional, trust and respect (as discussed earlier) will be included in it, so let loose with your ideas. Don't be surprised if some are rejected, and above all, don't be personally insulted. The reason for the rejection may not have anything to do with you or the idea. I once had two complete verses (melody and lyric) of what I thought was a great idea – 'Here I am in paradise/I'd rather be in love' – rejected by both Fred Knobloch and Thom Schuyler, *not* because they thought it was bad, but because a fellow staff writer of theirs had a song entitled 'I'd Rather *Fall* in Love.' Although that song was completely different from my idea, the titles were too similar and the other writer too close for them to feel comfortable working on my idea. I didn't argue with them. I thought they did the right thing.

While we're on the subject of rejection, it would be a good idea for you to learn to deal with it. You don't have to accept the implication of rejection – that your material is unworthy – but you should accept the fact that it's going to happen at every stage of the business, from collaborators, publishers, producers and artists to radio programme directors and record buyers. And it's going to happen a lot. One man's trash is another man's treasure, there is no accounting for taste, etc. Joe South tells the story of one of the most successful publishers in Nashville turning down one of his songs with the comment, 'What the hell is a boondock, anyway?' (The question was answered when Billy Joe Royal cut 'Down in the Boondocks.') More recently 'What's Love Got to Do With It' was turned down by at least one major artist before Tina Turner cut it – a major artist who happened to be Tina Turner.

So (if you can stand one more cliché) don't get mad, get even. But do it in a genteel way. If you have an idea you feel was wrongly rejected, get your revenge by proving that it was a good idea after all. The only way to do that is to turn it into a good song. File it away for another co-writer. (That is what I did with 'I'd Rather Be in Love,' and when I finally did get it finished, with the co-writing help of Pat Alger, we got it cut.) Or develop it a little more on your own and repitch it to the co-writer who originally rejected it. Or write it by yourself. When you get it cut and thus prove that you were right all along, your revenge will feel more like a boost of self-confidence and it will be much more sweet, friendly and productive than if you had lost control of your emotions and called a co-writer an imbecile. For right now, though, go on to your next idea.

Your co-writer certainly likes your next idea, but he really loves it after he changes one little word and consequently completely alters your original conception of the song. For example, imagine if Terry Britten said to Graham Lyle (or vice versa), " 'What's love got to do with it' sounds to me like a very cold statement emotionally, and it could be a turn-off to anyone who happens to be in love, but if we said '*Love,* love, *what* to do with it,' that would still fit perfectly with the melody. And it would express a more universal and positive emotion – the quandary of love." The song would have been radically different. You can expect alterations – along with editing and re-writing – to happen as often as rejection, because they are a part of the development process that continues until the final word and note of the final version are written. So get used to dealing with that, too.

Development, editing, rewriting – that's jumping ahead a bit. We're still at the basic idea stage, and here are some of the specific forms a song idea can take.

Title

If you jot down words, phrases or lines in your notebook or wherever you write song ideas down, the chances are that those will be *key* words, phrases and lines – titles. A title works as an idea if it tells you what the song is going to be about. 'Smoke Gets in Your Eyes,' 'Help Me Make It Through the Night,' 'Material Girl,' 'I'm So Excited,' – it's fairly clear just from the titles what these songs should say lyrically and what sort of music would best carry that message. A co-writer can see the whole song, or at least the range of possibilities, just from the title, and he can make an informed decision about whether he wants to pursue it or not.

On the other end of the title-as-idea spectrum, 'I Love You' isn't by itself an idea. It needs something more, like 'For Sentimental Reasons' or 'So Much It Hurts' or 'Just the Way You Are,' or a unique phrasing or a memorable melody – something out of the ordinary, something to catch the listener's attention. A title like 'Billie Jean' doesn't mean a thing at all standing by itself. Its particular euphonious quality aside, it's just a girl's name, like Marie or Sherry or Peggy Sue (all titles of major hits). Unlike 'Runaround Sue' or 'Bony Moronie,' which tell you something about the girls, you have to know something more than the names of the first four girls to know what the idea for the song is. The names could be just about anything as long as they sing right. The *ideas* for these songs are *not* the names, they are: 1) A one-night stand (Billie Jean) shows up at my door, accusing me of fathering her child; 2) 'You [Marie] are breaking my heart,' set to this beautiful melody; 3) Frankie Valli displays his amazing falsetto voice as he asks, 'Won't you [Sherry] come out tonight?'; And 4) 'I love you,' set to this new rock-and-roll rhythm, and it doesn't really matter what your name is [it was

Cindy Lou until Buddy Holly's drummer, Jerry Allison, suggested they use Allison's girlfriend's name, Peggy Sue] as long as it has three syllables and rhymes with *you* and *true*.

This is not to say that you don't have a song idea if you just have 'Marie, da da da daaah dah' or 'She-e-e-e-e-e-erry, bay-ay-by.' You just don't have a *complete* idea, and that's no reason to hold it back. Your co-writer might say, 'Marie what?' or 'Sherry what?' All you have to do is answer that − and both songs do in the very next line − and you're on your way.

First Line or First Verse

A strong first line can be as good a starting point as a title. If it's strong enough, it often *is* the title, as with 'In the Early Morning Rain,' 'Born to Lose,' and 'I Can't Stop Loving You.' As Dennis Morgan will explain in more detail later, the first line of 'I Knew You Were Waiting for Me' ('Like a warrior that fights') was written before the title, and it set the tone for the song. A first line as an idea should set a scene and, preferably, tell you where the song is headed. If it doesn't, then you should be able to add one more thought and get the point across. The title of 'The Christmas Song,' for example, never appears in the song and by itself gives you only the most general idea of what the song is about. It could easily have been written with the opening line 'Chestnuts roasting on an open fire' (by which it is, not surprisingly, better known) as the original idea. 'Vincent' could easily have started with its strong opening line and a description of a painting as its primary idea, while the idea of describing van Gogh the person was still in vague form.

Perhaps 'first line or first verse' should be amended to 'opening thought.' It may take an entire first verse to set the scene. If you don't have a hook or a title in mind, by the time you get to the end of the first verse, you should know what the chorus is going to do.

Even if your idea is just a phrase going nowhere, if you like the way it sounds, try it out on your co-writer. Maybe it'll spark something. That is, after all, what collaboration is all about. If not, file it away. Your co-writer, even if he doesn't have anything to add at the moment, may be as intrigued by the line as you are and may come up with something later on to complete the idea.

Chorus

The more complete your idea, the easier it's going to be to write the song. If you already have a chorus written − or even partially written − you've probably set up the song, or at least limited the possibilities to two or three. The verses should say and do certain things, melodically as well as lyrically, to support and lead into the chorus. Now it's just a matter of craftsmanship, a matter of filling in the blanks (which, granted, often proves to be the hardest part of writing a song).

This is what your co-writer wants to hear − an idea that's practically a song already. Make that a *good* song. It's a great feeling to be fired up by a good idea and have the song, complete with a set of directions, laid out for you. One possible problem inherent in this approach arises when your chorus idea is not quite right and you've developed it to a point from which, for you at least, there is no return. Your mind is locked in on it as it stands. It needs something else, and the burden will probably be entirely on the co-writer to come up with something to unlock the mind of the idea man.

The farther along a song has gone, the more work you've done on it and the harder it is to change. Even if you do have a concrete idea of lyrics and melody, you may want to leave the development of an idea open beyond a certain point in order to first get an unbiased, uninhibited reaction from your co-writer. See what his first impressions are. If you don't put your thoughts into his mind to start with, he may think of something better than what you had.

Riffs, Feels and Other Hunches

You've gone through all the ideas in your notebook and your co-writer has gone through all his. Nothing has generated a spark. As a last resort before starting from absolute scratch, he says, "Here's a little feel I've been playing around with." He plays about four bars worth of chord changes with an infectious rhythm and a 'push' here and there in the progression. It barely qualifies as even a fragment of a song idea, but it grabs you. ('I Knew You Were Waiting for Me' did not begin with the first lyric line, actually, but as a musical riff that became the melody of that first line.) And that's more than you can say about any of the other well-developed ideas that have been presented and rejected so far.

You say, "It sounds to me like the push – where it goes back to the I chord – is a natural spot for a nice little one-syllable title. It sounds like it wants to say 'Jump!' right there."

Your partner says, "Jump what? Like, 'I want to see you jump for my love?' "

Now you do have an idea (actually, the idea as well as the song belongs to David Lee Roth, Michael Anthony and Alex Van Halen), and you're off and writing.

It doesn't even have to be your own feel to serve as a take-off point. You might say, "I've been wanting to write a song like 'Rescue Me,' with a great R&B bass line. Here's the beat. Here's a new bass line . . . "

General Subjects or Story Lines

This is the lyric equivalent of the feel. One writer says to the other, "Let's write a honky tonk shuffle." Or a civil rights anthem, or a song about the new trend toward fidelity, or a song about a guy who defies his boss and ends up getting promoted for it, or a modern woman trying to reconcile the cold, competitive nature of her business life with the warmer, more traditional qualities of womanhood. You may not have a title or a melody, you may not know whether it's going to be verse-chorus or verses with a bridge, so it's probably now going to be one of those songs that writes itself in an hour. But opening the subject to discussion may evoke a key phrase that gets the song moving.

Overhauling Old Songs

You've got a song that you wrote five years ago. You've pitched it to everyone in town, to some of them more than once, and you have never got anything near a positive reaction. You still believe in the song, but you also believe in cash flow. So play the song for your co-writer, or maybe just the melody or the lyric alone, or maybe just the hook. In other words, omit the part you think is the weakest. The chances are that any objectivity you might have once had about the song has by now been overshadowed by bitterness at having it turned down so many times. Your co-writer may see something in a line or two that could liven it up, or he may see a completely different direction.

Of course, you're sacrificing some hard work. You've already written an entire song, and now you'll probably have to write even more, and you'll have to give up as much as half of it. If that bothers you, don't do it. What should bother you more is the fact that the song, despite its considerable (in your view) merits, is sitting on the shelf and is for all practical purposes dead. If the song has some unique personal value to you exactly the way it is, whether it gets cut or not, then by all means leave it alone. You've written it for reasons other than professional. Otherwise, let your wallet sit your ego down and have a heart to heart talk. And play the song for your collaborator.

It's more likely that you have a completed song but you know – either from your own objective analysis or from the comments of listeners whose opinions you respect – that your melody or your lyric should be stronger, or you need a bridge instead of a chorus. You've tried to rewrite, but you are too close to it. You're locked into one train of thought, and after a couple of tries, your heart's really not in it anymore. If the basis for a good song is there, try it out on a co-writer.

Do not, repeat, *do not* write a song with one co-writer and later offer it to a second co-writer, telling him, "I wrote this with Co-writer A, but his melody doesn't cut it. Can you do anything with it?" This will get you into big trouble with Co-writer A both legally and personally. That's not to say it can never be done. If the song qualifies as a dead song, and Co-writer A is no longer interested in reworking it, all you have to do is ask him if he minds if you show it to a third writer. If he does, then you don't. If it is a spur-of-the-moment action and the new co-writer is interested, then call Co-writer A before going any further. I've been in these situations several times, and they get sticky, even when they're completely above board. Here are some examples:

1. I was the third writer on a song that the other two writers had not developed beyond the title. Knowing that Writer A was involved, but that his contribution was only the title, I wrote the song with Writer B, who thought he could talk Writer A out of a full one-third percentage. Writer A insisted on the full share, so the remaining two of us each ended up with a third of the song for what was half the work. We didn't like it, but we didn't have any choice. The song was never cut anyway.

2. Jimbeau Hinson had a complete lyric that Michael Foster had written a melody for. Jimbeau and I, at a co-writing session, failed to interest each other with any new ideas, and Jimbeau pulled out his lyric, saying he wasn't knocked out by Foster's melody. He called Foster at that very moment to tell him exactly that (they had written together enough that Foster wasn't insulted by such a blunt comment) and to ask him if he minded if I took a shot at it. In other words, Jimbeau rejected Foster's melody and was going to give me the entire 50 percent melody share if I could come up with one that worked. Foster said he hadn't spent much time on it anyway and he agreed to withdraw his melody. As it turned out, I wasn't moved by the lyric and we went on to something else.

3. Steve Sanders (now with the Oak Ridge Boys) had a song that his producer, Tony Brown, thought needed to be rewritten. He had played it for Troy Seals, who said he would work on it. After some weeks, Brown hadn't heard

anything from Seals, and he asked me if I wanted to look at it, warning me at the same time that Seals did have it on his desk. A day or two later, I brought in a new lyric (with the title and original melody virtually intact), only to find that Seals had finally come up with something, and that because of his position, both in their company and as a well-known songwriter/artist, they were going with his version rather than mine. I was disappointed, of course, but I was aware of the situation ahead of time. There were certainly no hard feelings. I came out of it with some good lyrics that I might be able to use later on, along with the professional respect of the others involved. As far as I know, the song in question was never cut.

These three examples were chosen to illustrate one small point – the complications of using incomplete or unpublishable songs as ideas. But they also happen to represent three different types of co-writing relationships described earlier – equal, composer/lyricist and song doctor – as well as three different kinds of ideas to start from – a title, a lyric and an entire song. They give you an idea of the diversity of experiences that come under the heading 'collaboration.'

From Nothing With the many types of ideas and concepts to start (or finish) a song from, it seems unlikely that two writers could sit down to write and find nothing whatsoever of mutual interest to work from. But every once in a while, even if you both come in with a full page of song ideas, you and your partner work your way to the bottom of the page in a matter of minutes. Then you are faced with what is to most beginning collaborators the great professional nightmare – two writers completely dry of ideas, sitting there staring at each other, wondering what happens now.

Roger Greenaway will say in a later chapter that he and Roger Cook never got together until one of them developed an idea, but nowadays Greenaway travels to Nashville periodically for three weeks' worth of writing, armed normally with only about one week's worth of ideas. "I feel very badly if I go into a writing session with nothing in my head," he said. "I *don't* feel so badly if he says to me the first thing, 'I haven't got an idea in *my* head.' That's great because you're starting from base, and often times that's the time to write a hit, when neither of you has an idea. You just talk, relax, and from the talk comes a title. Or you might be strumming on the guitar and 'Hey, remember what you just did.' Or you might run the tape back, if you're doing that, and pick up on something. That's how it starts, the germ of an idea."

As Greenaway suggested, you and your co-writer may come up with better ideas, or ideas that you wouldn't have come up with alone, if your minds are completely open. Also, the chances of hitting on a mutually acceptable thought are likely to be better if that thought is developed together. For example, it might be easier to write an idea at 10.00 a.m. if it comes naturally out of two writers' collective mood at 10.00 a.m., as opposed to writing (again at 10.00 a.m.) an idea that reflects the mood one writer was in at a bar at closing time the night before, when he thought of the idea.

There is only one rule to remember when you're out of ideas: don't panic.

Talk. Play. Try a random chord change or rhythm or riff. Talk about whatever's on your mind, whether it's US foreign policy or the latest edition of *EastEnders* or your car's transmission problem. You've been dry of ideas before. Have a little self-confidence. Something will come up.

"Yeah," you say, "but when?" If a certain amount of time passes – half an hour, two hours, whatever – and you and your partner are now just staring silently at each other, one way out of it is to say, "All right. Who's cutting? Who needs a song?" In other words, make an assignment out of the writing session. Find out who's looking for songs. Most major publishers keep abreast of such things. If you don't have a publisher, check in the music press and with other writers. Pick an artist you like or one you have a good connection with. When you hear something like "The Oak Ridge Boys need two songs to go on a Greatest Hits album" (no joke, this really happened), it should spark at least one idea – the idea of all the money you'll make if you can write the right song for the Oaks, since the album title all but guarantees that the two new songs will be hit singles.

If you're not interested in writing for a specific artist, or if previous efforts to tailor-write songs have resulted in less-than-great songs, then think of a song that you like or wish you had written. Borrow from it. Turn the melody around. Twist the title into something different. Just make sure your changes are *substantial,* so that your song is distinct from (and does not legally infringe upon) the model.

Still nothing? No spark? I think this situation is unlikely unless your mind is on something other than songwriting to begin with. I can't recall ever coming out of a co-writing session with nothing whatsoever accomplished. Even if it took the entire session to hit on an idea or a melody or some fragment, there was always something to take home and work on and finish at a later session. If, however, your co-writing session has reached a dead end and you feel you've given it an honest and best effort, then call it a day. Maybe you weren't in the right mood. (That is not a very good excuse coming from a writer who considers himself a professional.) Maybe your co-writer wasn't. Maybe you and he are not going to be able to work together after all. Maybe you ought to wait and get together again when you have a sure-fire, developed idea.

CHAPTER EIGHT

MECHANICS OF
WRITING

Exactly what do you do when you sit down to write a song with another person? Well, you just sit down and write a song. I can't tell you how to think up a good lyrical line or a good melodic phrase. I can't tell you that if your partner comes up with the chorus, you should come up with the verse. I can't tell you why you can write a great song one day and a piece of trash the next. That is why songwriters are all 'bananas,' according to Cynthia Weil. "We earn a living doing something that we don't know how to do," she explains.

And Roger Greenaway adds, "If anyone really knew how to write a hit, they wouldn't tell you."

When I told my friends I was writing a how-to book on co-writing, the most common reaction was, "That's easy. One, learn to write. Two, find somebody to co-write with. Three, do it." Despite the flippancy, there is a worthwhile message implicit in these three easy steps to co-writing, and that is: if you can write, then you can co-write. When it comes to taking ideas and putting them into a form that rhymes and sings well, co-writing is pretty much the same as writing alone – except that you have help. There's no shortcut, no trick, no computer programme (yet), no aspect of co-writing that will allow you to bypass the fact that somebody – either you or your co-writer – has to think up a lyric and a melody. It's like building a house. You can do it all yourself, laying every brick and hammering every nail. Or you can build it with a partner. With a partner, *you* don't have to lay every brick or hammer every nail, but *somebody* has to. The walls of a house are not going to raise themselves, and the lines of a song are not going to rhyme themselves, just because two people are working on it instead of one.

One change you'll have to make when you work with a partner is to start thinking out loud. You're not making full use of your partner if you spend a half-hour in silence coming up with a complete verse and then offer it to him for comment. He should be involved in it as soon as you can put your concept for the verse into words.

Starting Off   When you write with someone for the first time, you're probably going to be a little nervous at the start – rather like you would be on a first date. That's normal, even for the pros. "Every song's the first one," Will Jennings says. "If it's with people you have an ongoing creative relationship with, it makes it a bit easier, but it's always the first song." In other words, you're supposed to be a little nervous. A good song idea will break the ice.

It may seem obvious to say this, but it is important: agree to proceed before proceeding. Make sure you're both working on the same song. Don't waste time working on an idea that your co-writer has already rejected, just because you still believe in it. Don't try to ram it into his ears, thinking he'll learn to like it if he hears it enough. If he keeps having to say to you, "Hold on, I thought we were writing this for Kenny Rogers, and you're writing lyrics for a woman to sing," stop and clear the air. If you're no longer thinking of Kenny Rogers, say so and say why. Take as much time as you have to talk out the idea. A clear idea may not be any easier to write, but it will be easier to co-write if both writers are focusing their efforts in the same direction.

While your writing alone may usually follow a certain pattern – your songs almost always start from a snatch of melody, for example, or a title – you should be prepared for anything when you're working with a collaborator. The possibilities are much more varied than lyric-first or melody-first techniques.

Some writers prefer to write top to bottom in order to get a natural flow of thoughts throughout the song. Once they have a title, they start with the first line and go from there to the second line. The scene behind the opening credits in the film *Ishtar* shows Dustin Hoffman and Warren Beatty doing exactly that, progressing line by line, with Hoffman often asking "What?" or "Why?" to key the next line. (For the sake of this discussion, ignore the fact that their songs, which were really written by Paul Williams and the film's director Elaine May, are absolutely awful.)

So writers like to get the chorus right first, since it's going to be the most important part of the song, then go to the verses. Others may outline the entire song, deciding what each verse is going to say, then write it as it comes, the easiest parts first no matter where in the song they happen to fit. Others like to write the last line of the verse first, to make sure the verses lead into the chorus. Or they may outline the verse with the rhyming words only – the last word in each line – before writing any complete lines. Jay Livingston recalls that his partner Ray Evans started 'Buttons and Bows' in a difficult place. "Ray's the one that came up with this: ' . . . While you keep on wearing those rings and things and buttons and bows.' That was the ending of the phrase, and I took a long time to write an opening to it. That's an awful way to write a song."

Development   "You've got to hammer it out, back and forth," says Dennis Morgan. Livingston says he and Evans would "argue our way through. Not heavy arguments. We'd work it out."

That's about as specific as the instructions get at this point. You have an extra mind, your co-writer's, at your disposal. Take full advantage of it. Get ideas moving back and forth between you.

And keep talking. If you've got a good start but still haven't decided where the song is going, or you're 'giving the idea its head' (like you would a race horse) to see where *it* wants to go, then make all your thoughts known. Don't be embarrassed to throw the most off-the-wall ideas into the discussion. "If it sounds dumb," Morgan says, "so what? Try something else." And, of course, don't be afraid to throw ideas right back out if they don't work. Questions that should constantly be asked are: "What are we trying to say here?" and "What does the song want to do or need to do here?" Once you've got the answers, all you have to do is write them down.

Getting Unstuck

You're halfway through a song, and suddenly it's just like writing alone again. Despite all the talk about how collaborators spur each other on, about one taking the lead when the other is stuck, you and your partner are now both drawing blanks for ideas. You are both stuck. Fortunately, there are a few ways to get unstuck with a collaborator that aren't available to the single writer.

As you did when you first sat down, start talking. Often when you're stuck, you'll notice you're both staring *silently* at your notepad. You're stuck for specific lines, but you probably have some ideas about what the next part should say and do. Get the back-and-forth going again with some conversation. Talk about anything.

If you're really stuck, take a break. Get some lunch. Make some phone calls. You and your partner don't necessarily have to break together. A few minutes of solitude may be all it takes to spark an idea.

Letting it Sit

Don't give up too easily – writing songs is not supposed to be easy work – but don't be afraid to call it a day. Sometimes you know you've reached a point of diminishing returns, where your mind is no longer fresh. You feel as though you could sit there for two more hours and not make any more progress. It's time to blow the whistle and recharge your creativity. I've found that for some songs, the mind-set of a verse may be different from the chorus, and switching from one to the other is difficult. The next morning, that second verse, the part that I spent two non-productive hours on the previous afternoon, comes pouring out as fast as I can write it down.

Sometimes it takes longer. Hal David and Burt Bacharach didn't feel 'What the World Needs Now' was quite right, and it sat around for three years before David finally took a new lyrical approach. Nickolas Ashford and Valerie Simpson also have let unsatisfactory songs sit for long periods of time. "The best way to handle the situation," says Simpson, "is to leave it and come back to it in six months or a year. Or maybe even two years later we need a piece of material and we'll remember that song we filed away. It's easy for us to finish it at that point because the time is right. Sometimes the time is just right to write a song and if you don't try and force it, a song will find its proper moment to come to life."

Unless you are involved in a solid, long-term writing relationship like David and Bacharach or Ashford and Simpson, you probably will *not* want to say to your co-writer, "Why don't we let this sit for a year." Overnight or a couple of days would be more like it. And if you do end your writing session on an unfinished note, try not to quit without mapping out the rest of the song. Have a clear idea of what it needs so that if you're thinking about it before the next session, your thinking will be on the right track.

You can also agree to work independently. I've done this many times when I became frustrated with my own contributions. If you're struggling for a melody, just say, "This melody's not so good. Let me work a while and get together tomorrow." Those are the exact words Jay Livingston says he often told his partner Ray Evans. Or if it's a lyric problem: "My mind's somewhere else right now. Let me take this home. I know exactly what we need to say here. I'll call you as soon as I get it."

A Co-writing Session

As you will see in Chapter 10, most writers have a hard time recalling exactly how their songs happened to be written. They can remember who had the original idea and maybe a line or two, but if it was a case of head-to-head writing, as opposed to lyricist and composer working alone, the writers more often than not say something to the effect of, "We just wrote it together from that point on."

Consequently, the only way to get a blow-by-blow account of a co-writing session is to listen in on one. What follows is a description of a writers' workshop session organised by the Nashville Entertainment Association. The idea was to write a song in two sessions – one for lyrics and a later one for melody. The co-writers in the first session were a panel of four hit songwriters – Don Pfrimmer, Kent Robbins, Tom Brasfield and moderator Peter McCann – plus a participating audience of about 50 songwriters. The following summary does not begin to capture the spirit and especially the humour of the two sessions, but it does illustrate some general points about the mechanics of collaboration and about songwriting in general.

In the first session, the first order of business was to find a song idea, and the audience submitted titles. 'What's Wrong With This Picture' was the one chosen. Immediately, Brasfield said his usual routine is to start describing situations, and he did so: "You might think, your typical somebody-done-somebody-wrong-and-they-didn't-end-up-together song, and then we could say a guy goes into a bar and he sees one of his ex-loves or his old flames and she pulls out a picture of her and her new family, and boom, you go into what's wrong with this picture and he talks about why it isn't happening."

After a few more related situations were suggested, Pfrimmer put the question back to the man who suggested the title. The idea man explained: "It struck me as a guy, he had just got over a divorce, he's cleaning out the closet or whatever, and he finds a picture of him and his wife on a honeymoon. What's wrong with this picture? Is there something missing here? What's hidden here that I didn't see that caused the problem now?"

The writers agreed that was a less obvious and more interesting way to take the song, and Robbins quickly came up with the images that would eventually be the opening lines. "I had the idea of a guy, maybe he's got everything," he said. "He's got two cars in the driveway, a big, beautiful house, a home and a family, and everything appears to be really cool. Everything's fine, but the light in his wife's eyes, that spark isn't there any more. When he sees his wife, the house, the kids, the job's great, but there's something missing. What's wrong with this picture?"

Pfrimmer noted that there were now two directions, two pictures: one was an overall view of the man's situation as Robbins described it; the other was an actual photograph. His observation set off a lengthy discussion that ended with an agreement to try to paint a picture of the man's life in the first verse, maybe introduce a physical photograph in the second, and *not* tip off the fact that something's wrong until the first line of the chorus (the title line).

From the point of deciding on a title, at least 20 minutes had gone by, and not a word or a note had been written. There had been nothing but talk, because the writers, Pfrimmer especially, wanted to have a clear idea of the song they were working on.

Finally, McCann said, "So we're looking for lines now." After several suggestions from the audience, Robbins suggested, 'Two stories/Two kids/Two cars in the driveway.'

While others were offering up more 'two' images and developing the idea to lead into *too* much or *too* little something, Robbins could be heard in the background working his three images into a singable metre. There were more discussions and more lines rejected from the audience, mostly because they didn't fit the plan that had now been agreed on. Then Robbins made a case for his line, suggesting that it be followed with a second positive image. McCann felt the line belonged somewhere else in the verse. More discussion. By now, Robbins had picked up his guitar, explaining that he just had to have it in front of him to write.

Thirty minutes into the session, Robbins again presented his opening line, with a simple three-chord melody: '(G) Two children /(Cmaj7) Two storey (D)house/ Two cars in the (G) drive.'

McCann went for it this time. "Now we have a metric framework in which to work, to come up with the second line of this verse, it feels almost natural that we should follow [the metre of the first line]," he said. "We have something to work with now. This is great."

Immediately, someone in the audience asked Robbins to sing the first line, and the audience member added a second: 'We earned it/ We had it all/We've finally arrived.' Line accepted. Robbins sang it through again, continuing after *arrived* to a C chord, saying it can't help but go to the C. Eventually, that is exactly where it would go.

Then, while McCann made a case for a different metrical arrangement for the next two lines, Pfrimmer was thinking about the last line of the verse, leading into the chorus. "I think it would be neat if you ended it with, like, 'It's just wonderful, and it's too good to be true,' " he said.

"Let's work backward from that," said McCann.

More discussion and suggestions. At one point, Pfrimmer tried to explain something and McCann said, "Could you *da* it out for me?" Pfrimmer responded with his metrical idea, set to the words *da da da da da*.

Robbins suggested a melody for the second half of the verse using the chord progression C, G(B bass), Am, D for the third line, then repeating the melody for the first two lines with this final lyric line: '(G) A wonderful (Cmaj7) picture/(D) Too good to be (G) true.'

The missing lines turned out to be extremely difficult to find, the main problem being that every suggestion – even the use of the word *picture* – seemed to give away the chorus. Other ideas were rejected because they played too cleverly on photographic terms, although one such – 'We captured the moment' – almost made it.

Point of view was temporarily accepted from an audience suggestion for the end of the third line, to rhyme with *true* in the last line. More discussion on whose point of view it is. An audience member suggested, 'It all looked so perfect/From my point of view.' A few minutes later, Robbins suggested as a solution to the problem of *picture* in the last line: 'Don't we look happy/Too bad it's too good to be true.'

That was it. Robbins sang it from the top.

> *Two children, two storey house, two cars in the drive*
> *We earned it, we have it all, we've finally arrived*
> *It all looked so perfect, from my point of view*
> *Don't we look happy, too bad it's too good to be true.*

It did, in fact, seem too good to be true – the first verse was finally complete, two-and-a-half hours after the session began. It was decided that since Robbins came up with a good melody, these same writers (rather than the originally planned team of melody writers) would complete the song at the next session.

Session Two was no easier. Working first on the chorus, Robbins picked up on an idea he had in the early part of the first session – something is gone from the picture. He suggested that 'The love is gone,' be the last line, the clincher, of the chorus. Line by line, the chorus began to take shape, and then, with time running out on the session, they got the second verse:

> (Chorus)
> *What's wrong with this picture*
> *It looked so good for so long*
> *Something is missing*
> *The love is gone*
>
> *Those memories, that photograph, still hangs on the wall*
> *The silence between us now, that says it all*
> *We got what we wanted, we lost what we had*
> *We were so happy, where did the good life go bad*

'What's Wrong with This Picture' © Copyright 1987 by the Nashville Entertainment Association, P.O. Box 121948, Nashville, TN 37212. All rights reserved. International copyright secured. Lyrics used by permission.

A few things to note about the writing of 'What's Wrong with This Picture':

First and foremost, you can see that songwriting is not easy for even the most successful writers. Because their personal standards are so high, it may actually be harder. While there were moments of inspiration in the writing of this particular song, they are out-weighed by the long stretches of hard work. That should give you a little bit of consolation the next time you're having a hard time with a song.

Before very much discussion went by about the title, Pfrimmer asked the man who had the idea what he had in mind. In other words, the total idea was not explained fully by the title. I'm sure the idea man is thankful for that opportunity, because the other concepts suggested by Brasfield and McCann were not exactly like his. If nothing happens with the song, he is less likely to say, "It was a good idea, but my co-writers missed it."

The writers spent a great amount of time talking about the idea in the beginning, when they might have just jumped right in. Their purpose in that was, of course, to make sure they were all working on the same idea, to try to avoid wasting time later. The writing took quite a long time even with the direction of the song clearly stated and agreed upon. It might have taken much longer had all the possible directions been *written* rather than talked out before they were rejected. Or the song might not have been as original, if one of the easier routes had been taken.

Several times Robbins suggested lines that were rejected or else received with indifference by his co-writers. Yet he kept bringing them up until they were accepted. Using tact rather than force, he made a slightly stronger presentation each time he offered them. The melody, in fact, appears to have originally been just an extra support device to help Robbins pitch one of his lines.

From Brasfield's absence after the opening part of this account, you might assume that his contributions were negligible. That would be an absolutely erroneous assumption. Remember, it was Brasfield at the beginning who jumped in and started the thoughts flowing, picturing some of the possible situations. It was Brasfield who suggested they try to interpret the 'picture' both ways – as an overall view of life and as an actual photograph. Even though he isn't quoted as often as the others, his contributions were just as valuable as anyone else's.

Some songs will take less time to write, some more, and none will be written in exactly the same way as 'What's Wrong with This Picture.' But all in all, this was a typical co-writing session.

CHAPTER NINE

REAL-ATIONSHIPS

I've been saying that there are as many different ways to write a song as there are songwriters, and now I'm going to show you with some real-life examples. Here is how some successful writers work.

Jay Livingston   Jay Livingston and Ray Evans won Academy Awards for 'Buttons and Bows' and 'Que Sera Sera,' and their music is still heard all around the world whenever the theme song to the TV series *Bonanza* comes on. They met at the University of Pennsylvania, where Livingston led a dance band that included Evans as first saxophone. When they first decided to be songwriters, they wrote at night, with Evans writing lyrics and Livingston doing melodies. After six years and a bit of success in New York, they moved to Hollywood. Writing on assignment for various studios, including a 10-year stint at Paramount, they kept regular office hours, beginning at 10.00 a.m.

"Here's how we write," Livingston said. "Ray writes a lot of words. Two pages he wrote on 'To Each His Own,' trying to make it mean something. And I saw one line, 'Two lips must insist on two more to be kissed,' And I write . . . [sings the melody for that line]. Then I go on and write the melody. And then we start over.

"I think that's why I write songs that have lasted so long, because the melodies are strong . . . And these melodies are strong because I wrote them first as melodies. Then we went back and wrote the words. And we'd do that all the time. Now on a rhythm song, I might write the melody to some words . . .

"Ray's an early riser. He writes in the morning, and we get together in the afternoon to work. Now at the studio I had to be in there at ten o'clock in the morning, which drove me crazy. We had our first Oscar, I started coming in at eleven. And we had our second Oscar, I started coming in at noon. They didn't like it, but they didn't say anything. I came in at quarter to twelve, we'd talk about it, then we'd have lunch. Then in the afternoon we'd write a song. That's what I like to do. I like to stay up late and work late."

Dave Loggins   For a three or four-year period in the mid-eighties, songs from MCA Music in Nashville were all over the American country charts. Hits came from a staff that included Loggins, Don Schlitz, Russell Smith and J. D. Martin, working in various combinations. Loggins recalled the scene:

"We came in every morning about nine-thirty, and it became a chemistry because of co-writing, a oneness between six or seven people here. And co-writing was the absolute hub of that whole wheel. It was because everything was so interwoven. One day I'd write with Don, one day with J. D., one day I'd write with Russell. One week, whatever. There were about six or seven writers here for that three-year frame. We were all here every day about nine-thirty unless somebody was ill. At nine-thirty, ten, people were downstairs getting coffee. Then we just adjourned to different rooms.

"The term 'work' didn't come into play. It was like fun. And it was exciting, man, because we were all like a chemistry of one, as opposed to one person. It was as if everybody, they know how good they are, and it was like 'My God, what are we gonna do next!' They couldn't wait to see what was going to come out of each other next. And you were given the reciprocal kind of energy, the abilities, the fusion of all that.

"We worked, as I recall, in week time-frames. Sometimes it spilled over. I think J. D. and I worked one week and then some the next week. Don and I might work two or three days, because he's so fast, and he may have already something booked on Thursday and Friday. It just seemed to work. If I was supposed to work with Don when I was finishing some stuff with J. D., which happened, he'd do some other things, or vice versa, he'd spill over into me, I'd do other things."

Unlike the classic co-writing teams of two or three writers, at MCA there was no permanent team. "The preference I had was co-writing with *them* – any one of them – in the building," Loggins said. "I didn't like to go out of the building. There wasn't really any favourite. What I liked was I got a different input from J. D. than I did from Don or Russell or anybody. J. D. and I wrote a different type of song than Don and I did – much more to the r&b side, grooves. Don and I wrote basically country 2/4s and stuff. And Russell and I, the stuff we'd do would be a little more Memphis-sounding."

The styles weren't the only variation from one co-writer to the next. Loggins's responsibilities also changed to fit the co-writer. For example, with Schlitz, a fast lyricist, Loggins concentrated more on music. But with Martin, he found himself handling a good portion of the lyric work. "It's not really a responsibility," Loggins said. "That's just the way it turns out. There are others that have a much more brilliant lyrical approach, so you don't have to weigh so heavy on yourself lyrically, so you can think more melodically. I like all of it, because it all will work. You don't have to move far from one position to another."

In such a stimulating atmosphere, Loggins found that he didn't necessarily need to come into a co-writing appointment with an idea. "It didn't really matter. What we found was that as we became very regimented to the schedule, if I was working with Don one week and J. D. was not working the next week, I may be walking by J. D.'s office and hear him playing something and ask him what it was. And I'm working with him next week, so he just holds on to it. It could start that way. J. D. and I might be working and we might go in and not have anything. There seems to be so much less of a negative thought pattern when you're going to co-write with somebody on that level. It's as if you seem to know that all you have to do is get in the room and play for a while and somebody'll play some little chop and you'll be off and running. It's kind of a melodic idea and eventually a lyrical thing, whatever. Don and I have gone in with just a thought or something, just started spinning it around. Before you know it, we're playing something.

"The most significant factor was the positive energy, man. Whether you had an idea or a piece of something or you had nothing, it was going to happen. It was inevitable that it would happen. With co-writing. Now on the other hand, if I come in now in the morning at nine-thirty or ten, I'm going to be working on something by myself. I'm just not sure how long it's going to take.''

Roger Greenaway

Roger Greenaway started in music as a singer in the English quartet the Kestrels in the early sixties. When one of the members quit, Greenaway recruited his former schoolmate from Bristol, Roger Cook. Another personnel change dimmed the group's future, as far as Greenaway could see (he says he has always been the pessimist). He had had one bit of success on his own as a songwriter – a Petula Clark cut – and he knew some people in the London music business as a result of The Kestrels' success, so he suggested to Cook that they try to write together. Fifty minutes after they got together for the first time, they wrote 'You've Got Your Troubles, I've Got Mine,' which The Fortunes recorded and which sold more than two million records worldwide. Cook moved from Bristol to London, where the team continued writing, and later producing ('My Baby Loves Lovin'' for White Plains) and recording (they had a US hit as David and Jonathan with The Beatles' song 'Michelle').

Once they began writing together, Greenaway never wrote alone again. "It was clear that whenever Cook and I got together, he was my catalyst, and I guess I was his," Greenaway explained. "There would be many, many times in the next seven or eight years where we would have written songs on our own which were three-quarters to 80 percent finished, but what would happen is, I'd play him what I'd finished, he'd play me what he'd finished, and the other would 'knock it into shape.' So even though we were not always writing one-on-one, I felt that he was always influencing what I was doing and vice versa.

"We never went every day to the office and said, 'I'm going to write today.' It was ritually, wait until somebody had an idea. And generally, if he had an idea, he would develop it to a great extent, and I'd do the same. It was the finishing off that was the thing between us, where the one could see the wood for the trees, so to speak. Cook had a great ear for things like that. You could start something off, and before you knew where you were, he had it finished."

Both writers wrote music and lyrics, although Greenaway says Cook was the better lyricist. Their partnership was so successful that regardless of their individual contributions to a particular song or production, the credit was always 50-50. "I don't care if it was a name [a title]," Greenaway said, "as far as I'm concerned, it was worth it. That was a chemistry that always worked with anything we did, whether we did it together or semi-together or even separately. We did a lot of production separately, except we always came together at the mixing stages. We had this partnership. We shared. Everything had Cook and Greenaway's name on it. It was an established name. It was crazy not to use it."

During the last two years of their partnership, Greenaway and Cook began working separately with other writers, but even in those cases their partnership was maintained in the song credits. "If it really was a finished song, and the other guy [Greenaway or Cook] could do nothing more, as far as I'm concerned my partnership was with Cook and not that particular writer, and he the same with me. So we would split it, our share, half [25% each for Greenaway and Cook], and the other guy would get his half. So it wasn't like a third-third-third if that was the way it worked. But if it was the three of us, of course we shared it three ways."

The partnership ended when Cook decided to move to Nashville. Greenaway began working with other collaborators, which he said was a different experience in only one sense. "I have never ever found the magic with other people that I had with Cook – at least I don't think so. I've had hits, but I've never found that flow, that magical flow we seemed to have together. However, if you said to me 'What was it like writing with him [another writer] and writing with him?' I'd have to say it's no different writing with any *professional* songwriter. Any guy worth his salt writes basically the same way. We all like to start with a nucleus of an idea, an idea for a title. Words suggest melody – certainly to a songsmith they do – and you might not be able to take it anywhere, so you say, 'I've got this piece of a song' and play it, and they go, 'It's here.' And he's going somewhere already and he's inspiring you. It's what I call 'bouncing off.' "

Richard Rodgers The most convincing argument for being flexible in your work habits is Richard Rodgers. Probably the most successful of all Broadway composers, Rodgers enjoyed productive partnerships with two men who were opposites both personally and professionally.

With Lorenz Hart, Rodgers would usually write the melody first and Hart would then write the lyrics, starting with what Hart termed "the most distinctive melodic phrase" and then expanding around that. It is likely that many of their songs would never have been written had not Rodgers started them, because Hart hated to work. Rodgers was a mild-mannered individual and a disciplined melody writer who would block out a certain amount of time each day to work. Hart was a party animal, irresponsible about business appointments, and a nervous, restless writer whose lyrics often came in furious spurts. Toward the end of their partnership, Rodgers had to rewrite some of Hart's lyrics because Hart was nowhere to be found.

Oscar Hammerstein II, who followed Hart as Rodgers's lyricist, was the exact opposite of Hart in personality and in his working method. Before they wrote anything down, they would spend hours at a time talking out a show. Then Hammerstein would retire to his farm in Bucks County, Pennsylvania, to write lyrics, working slowly and painstakingly, often spending weeks on a single song. He followed a daily regimen that had him at his writing desk by 9.30 a.m. and in bed by midnight. He wrote standing up at an old bookkeeper's desk (a gift from Jerome Kern), and he tested his lyrics with dummy melodies – *awful* dummy melodies, according to his wife. Rodgers then wrote the music.

They could hardly have written in the same room if they had tried, since Rodgers was as fast as Hammerstein was slow. (Ironically, Rodgers was the exact opposite of Hammerstein's former partner Jerome Kern, who wrote melody first, worked when the spirit struck him, and would often strip down to his undershirt and literally sweat out a melody as Hammerstein patiently stood by.) For *South Pacific*, Rodgers wrote the melody to 'Bali Ha'i' in five minutes, and he got up from a sickbed to spend 20 minutes writing 'Happy Talk.' Though melodies had always come easy to him, he attributed his speed to Hammerstein's skill as a lyricist. The lyrics were so well crafted, Rodgers said, that all he had to do was put them on the piano and the melodies would write themselves.

Pam Rose, Mary Ann Kennedy and Pat Bunch

Kennedy met Rose at Pete Drake's publishing company in Nashville. Kennedy had been writing with Don Goodman (primarily a lyricist), and when Rose was signed to a record deal, Drake suggested they try writing together. "We realised how we complemented each other's musical styles," Kennedy said. "Plus we were singing sessions and we were just into a musical niche where we were just flowing with it. And I realised again that Pam would sometimes enhance my stuff by making it a little less mainstream. I'm real commercial-minded, and Pam sometimes tends to be a little bit more esoteric. What we can do alone is really, really good and sometimes great, but it was consistently great when we did it together."

Rose and Kennedy not only wrote together, they performed together in the all-woman country group Calamity Jane. In trying to write for the group, they decided they needed lyrical help, and through the suggestion of a BMI executive, they were put in contact with Pat Bunch. They spoke on the phone and even exchanged some lyrics and tapes but did not meet face to face until some time later.

True to their initial contact, they still seldom get together. Bunch lives twenty-five miles north of Nashville, and Rose and Kennedy live almost that far south and southwest, respectively, so many of their co-writing sessions are done over the phone. "Lots of people in Nashville get together and hammer it out," Bunch said, "and we don't do that. That's not the way we write. I don't feel like I do well in that situation because it takes me a long time to think about things. Usually I'm pretty confident that if I'm thinking about it myself I can examine more thoughts than I can if I'm with somebody."

Bunch feels that she and her partners are disciplined enough and self-motivated enough that the normal scheduled appointment approach is unnecessary. Kennedy describes that approach as a "building block process," in which a song is written by joint effort, line by line. Their approach is the opposite. Rather than each having equal responsibility for the entire song, each has an *area* of responsibility that corresponds to her strength. Basically, Bunch is the main lyric writer, and Rose and Kennedy handle the music. Ideas start from any of the three strengths. "It can start from a complete lyric that Pat has," Rose said, "with a musical hook or a feeling that Mary Ann has, or it can start from a chord progression that I have." At the end of a song, Kennedy's sense of commercialism is the strongest of the three, so her instincts usually carry most weight at that point.

But it is more complicated than that, because the responsibilities – or strengths – go beyond the mechanics of writing. As Rose explained, "We do *write* songs, but we *hear* records, so I've thought at times that we do write records." So while Kennedy and Bunch may be at their homes obsessed with an elusive melody and lyric, respectively, Rose may be experimenting with a reverb unit or programming a drum machine, developing technical skills that will prove vital once they get to the demo stage of the song.

John Lennon and Paul McCartney

The two front men for The Beatles began co-writing not long after they first met, when they were barely into their teens. From the beginning, they had their own performing group as an outlet for their material. Early in their relationship, they agreed to put both their names on all their songs.

Lennon once claimed they never wrote in the same room together, but in a book-length interview for *Playboy* several months before his death in December 1980, he recanted. He admitted that a lot of The Beatles' early hits were written with he and McCartney "playing into each other's noses." They wrote together, he added, because of the tremendous demand on them for material. Some of the products of that nose-to-nose writing are 'From Me to You,' 'I Want to Hold Your Hand,' and 'She Loves You.'

Like many co-writing teams, they each had an area of expertise, or at least *perceived* expertise. Lennon was perceived by McCartney to be the stronger lyricist because he was faster, although Lennon said that McCartney *was* capable of writing good lyrics but didn't always try hard enough. Lennon perceived McCartney to be stronger musically. After all, McCartney's superior knowledge of music was the reason they became friends and partners in the first place. Lennon said his own early musical contribution amounted to injecting blues influences and discordant sounds into McCartney's melodic ideas.

Despite Lennon's contention that they did in fact write many of their songs together, when he goes through them song by song, he tends to separate them, considering each song either his or McCartney's – even many of the early tunes. Whether he's talking about the original idea or the entire song is not always clear. When he does elaborate, it appears that they helped each other finish songs – helping with the middle or the bridge – more often than they sat down and started songs together. McCartney started 'We Can Work It Out' and Lennon helped with the 'middle eight'; vice versa on 'In My Life.' One song, 'Baby You're a Rich Man,' was originally two separate songs – one from each writer – shoved together.

Their relationship, as described by Lennon, seems to have been more competitive than cooperative – another indication that they did not do much collaboration in the usual sense of the word. Lennon talks of McCartney's writing 'Eight Days a Week,' which was the original title of their movie *Help*. Lennon then one-upped his partner by writing 'Help,' and by doing so knocked McCartney out of not only the single, but also out of the title song of the movie.

Lennon said that there was no resentment between the two of them over this sort of thing, and the only explanation for that must be that they shared royalties on all songs. Among the songs Lennon says he wrote alone are 'Strawberry Fields,' 'Nowhere Man,' 'Day Tripper,' 'Revolution' and 'Give Peace a Chance.' McCartney's songs include 'Hey Jude' 'All My Loving,' 'Yesterday,' 'Here, There and Everywhere' and 'Let It Be.'

Mick Jagger and Keith Richard

The writing team that is the song source for The Rolling Stones reluctantly started co-writing on the orders of their manager, Andrew Loog Oldham, after their first album hit. Oldham convinced Richard that if you can play an instrument, you can write a song. Richard, the Stones' guitarist, wrote the music, and Jagger, the lead singer, wrote the lyrics – sort of. Even though Jagger knew only a few basic guitar chords and could play piano with only one finger, he nevertheless contributed to the melodies that were developed from Richard's chord progressions. And according to Jagger, Richard wrote more lyrics than he is usually given credit for, and he seldom gave Jagger an instrumental riff without also giving him a title or a verse or some kind of lyric idea to work from.

Will Jennings

Will Jennings cut his teeth in Nashville in the early seventies, contributing both music and lyrics in a three-man songwriting team with Troy Seals and Don Goodman. After moving to Los Angeles in 1974, he worked on an album project with Tom Jans, still writing both lyrics and music. Then his publisher showed some of his lyrics to Richard Kerr, and an introduction was arranged. The first song they wrote was 'Somewhere in the Night.' Jennings recalls that he may have written a bit of the chorus melody to that song but that their responsibilities were usually split along the lyric/melody line. ''Richard's style was so fully formed and so distinctive and fresh to me, to my ears, that there was nothing to do musically, just get into the lyric,'' he explained. Even so, they usually wrote face-to-face. Ironically, both writers now prefer a secluded atmosphere to write in. (Kerr has said that if a collaborator arrives when he is in the middle of developing melody, ''Then they have to go out into the garden or into the bedroom. I can't have them walking around.'')

''In the early days,'' Jennings said, ''we would sit in the same room and really bleed. Later on I found I was more comfortable if there was a piece of music that I liked through and through, I would get it on cassette in some fashion and take it away with me and work. And that's generally the way I work. It seems like it goes faster.''

Originally, Jennings met with Kerr twice a week, but as his reputation grew, he was invited to work with other writers on specific projects. One of those was a song for The Crusaders' first recording with a vocalist. His collaboration with the group's pianist, Joe Sample, on that song ('Street Life') led to two albums of material (with Sample) for B. B. King. To write those albums, Jennings said, ''We just sort of went away for a couple of weeks and worked.''

Partly on the strength of that work, he was asked to collaborate with Steve Winwood. On those projects (four albums so far), he goes to Winwood's mansion, where Winwood has a studio and an area for Jennings to seclude himself and write lyrics.

His working arrangements differ with each collaborator and each song, Jennings explained, but with Kerr, Sample and Winwood – his three most successful partnerships – there is a normal pattern. He is given the music, often without even a title to work from (he wrote the lyrics to 'Higher Love' and the majority of his work with Winwood that way). ''If I really love the melody and really feel it, I usually get something,'' he said.

''In most cases in the past several years, if I'm writing from a piece of music, I'll have the whole piece of music, and I usually don't change a note. That's the way on 'Well You See a Chance,' which I wrote to the track 'Street Life,' and 'Somewhere in the Night.' One exception is Winwood's hit 'Back in the High Life Again,' which was a complete lyric by Jennings set to music by Winwood.

Jennings said he usually does not change a note of the composer's melody, because none needs changing. "Each one of those guys is a master in his own way, for his own kind of music, so there's not much to be done," he explained. "Maybe once in 20 or 30 songs I suggested some arrangement things. On a song called 'One Day I'll Fly Away,' which was a hit in Europe for Randy Crawford – it was a follow up to 'Street Life' – I just felt what Sample had for a verse should be a chorus and vice versa. You're dealing with a musician of enormous inspiration and calibre when you're dealing with a Joe Sample or a Steve Winwood or a Richard Kerr. So it might be an arrangement of this and that, but generally there's not that much to do except to try to write a lyric as good as the melody or give them a lyric that will inspire them to write something good."

Jennings has lately been writing with Rodney Crowell and working face-to-face, writing both lyrics and music again.

Nickolas Ashford and Valerie Simpson

This husband-and-wife team met in the early sixties in a Harlem church when Simpson was still in high school. Several years after they began writing together, they were discovered by the Motown writing team of Holland, Dozier, and Holland. They found that the highly competitive atmosphere at Motown resulted in speed as well as quality in their work. Among their hits from that period are 'Ain't No Mountain High Enough' and 'Ain't Nothin' Like the Real Thing.'

Simpson described their work method in an interview: "I write the music and Nick writes the lyrics, but he contributes to the melody and I to the lyrics. And it happens different ways every time, which is what makes it so much fun."

Their temperaments are different, Ashford said. "Sometimes Valerie can't go on unless she's really hot. Me, I can beat it out for three to four hours. But Val has to be really hot on the tune. She has to be inspired differently, but then we all get our inspiration in different ways.

"One thing we don't try to do is try to make it happen. When you try, that's the hardest. We keep it always relaxed and it feels good like that."

Once they get involved in a song, either one is liable to suddenly pour forth with music or lyrics. Simpson is an accomplished pianist and Ashford says he always has to have a tape recorder on while she plays so as not to miss any ideas. Ashford's lyrics also come the same way. "Sometimes I'll play and it's like he's in a trance," Simpson said. "He'll sing a whole verse right off the top of his head. I mean he rhymes, reveals the message, and structures a story straight out of his head . . . like 16 bars worth . . . which leaves me sitting there with my mouth open hardly able to believe it."

Ashford's piano skills are rather basic, but that limitation turns out to be useful also. "I can't stand to play the same thing over and over," Simpson says. "Nick hasn't studied as long so he can play four chords all night long without growing bored. The result is that he'll keep hearing something different. He'll draw many possibilities from the same four chords."

Hal David Lyricist Hal David and his composer partner Burt Bacharach had been writing with various collaborators in the Brill Building when a publisher suggested they work together. That was in 1957 in the Paramount publishing office. They had a few cuts, and then they were able to secure a record deal (with themselves as producers) for their favourite demo singer Dionne Warwick, the result of which was a decade of hits in the sixties, including 'Walk on By,' 'A Message to Michael' and 'Alfie.'

There was no formula, no set approach to their writing. When David published a book of his lyrics in 1968, he divided it into three sections: 'Sometimes the Words,' 'Sometimes the Music' and 'Line by Line – Measure by Measure.' The first two sections refer to songs in which the words came first and the music came first, respectively, but for the songs in the third section, David wrote, "When I say 'Line by Line – Measure by Measure,' I mean I don't really know how we started the song. We just got into a room and bounced ideas off each other. When we finally got an idea, either lyrical or musical, which excited both of us, we would then begin to write the song and pound it out line by line."

In an interview for the book *In Their Own Words,* David described his work habits: "If I'm working in the city I'll start at ten, ten-thirty. Mostly I like to work at home. It's easier. I have an office in the back where I have everything I need. I sort of walk around the house – I don't lock myself in the office. I work with a pencil and a yellow legal pad. I only type when I'm finished."

By the late seventies, David and Bacharach had split, and David began dividing his time between working with other melody writers, serving as president of ASCAP, and playing tennis. At that time, he revealed that despite the variety of ways he and Bacharach developed songs, he did in fact have a preferred approach, although it had changed over the years. "I used to prefer writing the lyric first," he said. "I felt I could structure the song. I'm equally comfortable either way. Lately I tend to prefer the music first because that motivates me."

Dennis Morgan For a five-year period beginning in the late seventies, Dennis Morgan and Rhonda (then 'Kye') Fleming wrote a string of hits that made them both millionaires. Their publisher, Tom Collins, produced Barbara Mandrell, Ronnie Milsap, Sylvia, and Steve Wariner, and thus they had a number of direct outlets for their songs. Morgan had been co-writing with other writers on Collins's staff. "Kye just walked in one day," he recalls. "We clicked right away.

"We wrote every day. By this time I'd already been co-writing a long time, had a great understanding of songs, I really did, from knowing probably a thousand bar songs, which is one hell of an education. Kye would often come up with the idea, and I would often add to, you know, do more of the music. Except that I think my strong point has always been the overall picture, like where things should go.

"That was true collaboration, because she'd do music with me, I'd do words with her, she'd do words with me and I would do music with her. It was constantly back and forth.

"Tom came up with a lot of those ideas, too, in the early years especially. He steered us and directed us and taught us a hell of a lot about the marketplace and about making a living as professional songwriters. But as it kept developing, we'd all come up with stuff, man, we'd all have ideas. Things would just fly in all over the place all the time because it was such a creative atmosphere. We'd experiment, we'd try different things, you know, let her fly. Just try to stay as active as we could on a daily basis."

Part of their routine was to start with a clear mind. "We would pray before we'd write – we're both spiritual people – really try to thank the Lord for everything that was going on and open the channel, get all the crap out of our lives and just open the channel to the real inspiration."

The inspiration was exploited, of course, by the high degree of craftsmanship Morgan and Fleming reached in the course of their five years together. Toward the end of their relationship, Morgan says, "It was so easy it scared me to pieces that it was so easy, compared to it being so difficult in the first five years of being in Nashville. By that I mean that somebody would say something and we'd make it a song. And it would make sense. We worked and we learned that you can take just about anything. You simply have to craft songs."

When Morgan and Fleming split, Morgan began collaborating with Steve Davis, and to complement Davis's melodic strength, Morgan now concentrated more on lyrics. "I applied what I'd learned lyrically to Steve's feels and melodies," he said. "I helped him edit his music; he would help me edit my lyrics – that, of course, being the whole art of collaboration, back and forth . . .

"You've got to get down, in and funky, and you've got to hammer back and forth. It never ends. You've got to hammer these songs out with the help of your collaborator. I've never had success with just writing a melody to a lyric or just writing a lyric to a melody. I can't do that. There's no soul in that approach to me."

Again, Morgan couples the 'soul' or the 'inspiration' with craftsmanship. He explained, "I've gotten it down now, I swear, I can meet a total stranger – I just did it in Los Angeles 11 times over a period of two-and-a-half weeks – walked into a room with total strangers and walked out with songs."

Felice and Boudleaux Bryant

Georgia-born Boudleaux Bryant was a classically trained violinist, but it was as a travelling country fiddler and guitar picker that he met Felice, who had grown up singing in her home town of Milwaukee. They married and moved to Moultrie, Georgia. To ease the boredom of daily life in a small town, Felice revived her childhood hobby of writing poetry and song lyrics. Boudleaux made them into songs by setting them to music. Fred Rose, the legendary songwriter and publisher who developed the career of Hank Williams, brought the Bryants to Nashville.

Though their relationship flourished romantically as well as professionally up until Boudleaux's death in 1987, they did have different temperaments and work habits. Felice wrote something every day, as she revealed in an interview in the seventies. "I will put at least one sentence down," she said, "sometimes a paragraph, or maybe just a bridge, but I do have a complete thought and I will write it down."

Boudleaux elaborated: "Felice has more of a compulsion to write than I do. I can go for six months and not write anything more than a note: 'I've gone down to the lake and I'm fishing.' . . . As far as my creative urge is concerned I do sit down and write my own music. I sit around and play my guitar, just thinking in my head and resolving something in my head that I'm going to forget tomorrow.

"I write constantly in my head and forget it, while she writes constantly and puts it on paper. She has enough lyric material to satisfy . . . 20 collaborators . . . To some extent I kind of feel it is my obligation to rise up occasionally to these wonderful ideas she has. My way of working is limited in a sense. I work on what I like or what I think will sound good on record. If it doesn't fall into that small category, I don't want to work on it to the extent of getting out a piece of paper and writing it down."

The Bryants' description of themselves makes them seem to be the classic picture of collaboration – the disciplined, hard-working lyricist and the carefree, naturally-inspired composer. But Felice's story of the Everly Brothers' hit 'Take a Message to Mary' (one of 27 Everlys' cuts the Bryants had) shows how closely they did work together. "I was at home when the idea for the song hit me," she said. "I had to call Boudleaux down at Acuff-Rose [their publisher] and sing the melody to him over the phone so he could write it down. I had the lyrics, but I knew by the time he'd get home I'd change the melody. Invariably, if a melody isn't that strong I'll change it during the day. Thank God he had it on paper. Not only had I changed the melody, but I'd gotten away from the metre. So he went to work on it, wrote some more lyrics and threw it all back into metre."

Bob Morrison   After two years in New York and six in Los Angeles, Bob Morrison moved to Nashville in 1973. Within a year, he had a hit, 'The River's Too Wide' by Jim Mundy, which Morrison says was probably the last time he wrote a complete lyric. "I came to see I had a melodic facility – I could write a lot faster melodically – so I was always ending up with half-finished songs, which was tremendously frustrating," he said. As a newcomer in town, Morrison had not yet developed enough co-writing relationships to provide the quantity of songs he wanted to produce, so he began working by post – with lyricists he already knew and with the hopeful song-writers who sent tapes to the publishing company.

The Combine Music postbag was the source of one of his best-known songs, 'Looking for Love,' as well as the Dickey Lee hit 'Angels, Roses and Rain,' but on the whole, it has not proved to be a very good source, Morrison said. Most of the songs that come in are written by amateurs whose work is simply "not up to par," he explained. "Yet something about an unopened package addressed to me, it's really difficult for me not to open it. Hey, the next Bob Dylan may be sitting out there."

Morrison tries diligently to get back to his potential co-writers within two to four weeks, and as he said, his answer is usually no. But when a lyric does grab his interest, he asks the writer to give him an exclusive shot at the song. Then, he says, "Something has to happen on the guitar." Exactly what happens? "The lyric will begin to speak to me . . . Once I've got a groove going, then I'll look at the lyric and say, 'Okay, does this go from A to Z?' I have to get the melody and think that we've got a song before we go any farther on it." At that point, "When we have a hook to hang the hat on," Morrison tells the lyricist. Then it becomes a "batting back and forth," rewriting lyrics if necessary, and otherwise polishing the song.

Despite his practice, Morrison's preferred work habits are like those of most co-writers. "I think it's better to sit in a room with a professional writer, eyeball-to-eyeball, and make decisions right there," he said. "It takes more time to send something back by post than it does to sit in a room with a professional writer who knows what you're talking about. I wouldn't advise [writing by post] for somebody, is what I'm saying. I got trapped into it a few years ago."

CHAPTER TEN

REAL SONGS

Allen Toussaint was once asked how he wrote songs. He answered, "To explain writing songs, oh . . . I'd have to write a song to explain it." This is how some hit songwriters 'explain it.'

'I Knew You Were Waiting for Me' by Dennis Morgan and Simon Climie, recorded by Aretha Franklin and George Michael.

Morgan met Climie at Stringfellow's bar in London, through a friend at Climie's publisher, Chrysalis. Morgan had just written 21 songs in three weeks with various co-writers, "just looking for something that clicked," he said. He felt that something when he met Climie and extended his trip a day to write. They met a year later in Los Angeles for a second song. A year after that they got together in London.

The title of their third song together, 'I Knew You Were Waiting for Me,' "just came out of the air," Morgan recalled. "We got together in a room, me with an acoustic guitar and a yellow legal pad; he had his piano and drum machine, and a few ideas written down on a piece of paper, an entire day to ourselves, nothing to do, which is very important. No schedules. Very important element to successful writing I think, away from telephones, knowing that there's no obligation that night, nothing, just free time. And that gets the juices going. I swear, it's like you're a kid again on summer vacation and you can go run through the field, go fishing and do any damn thing you want, and mentally I believe it's the same thing. It is for me.

"So anyhow, Simon would get a feel going, a drumbeat, play some chords. We'd start kicking things around. And very fast, when it starts happening, it starts happening. And I don't exactly know where this thing first started to take shape. I think we had some of the first verse. 'Like a warrior that fights.' Not the words, but I think he was doing a rhythm, a phrasing like 'da da da that fights, da da da da da,' just doing something like that. And I think the verse started first, but only little things, like 'Like a warrior that fights.'

"I'm good at just letting my mind drift. When you know you have nothing to do you can just drift, and it's so much fun, and all of a sudden this thing started coming together and the title came to me. 'I Knew You Were Waiting for Me.' And I felt like it was something there definitely. But we both thought, 'I don't know about it. I don't know if that's a real strong title or not.' But I felt that it was. The more I looked at it the more I felt that it was. And I started fighting for it, you know. This is it.

"It hit me right then that it was just perfect. I saw the whole thing, you know. And in the case of the lyric, Simon helped me a lot, too, in terms of coming up with different things. 'Crippled emotionally,' things like that. I'd get it going, but again, I'm real excellent at putting it in the little slot, exactly what it needs to say.

"Inside that title I did see how the elements could fight, which is the key to any good writing, I think – contrast and conflict, problems. So in those verses immediately I started seeing images like, 'It's a war, but I made it.' That simple, really, is that song, which is really, if you think about it, a three-act play. 'It's a war out there, but I made it back, because of you. I knew you were waiting for me, never gave up, here we are, and son of a gun.'

"And that's how I write these days, really, is try to find the conflict in something. The three-act thing, how the conflict comes in the beginning, how you beat it – it just all started falling together. So the verses all started falling out.

"The line, 'Somehow I made it to da da da da, *wo-oh,*' we had that differently, and he came up with this 'wo-oh, *oh-oh-oh,*' just stretched it out a little so we could say a little bit more. And again that entered into the play approach to songwriting and giving you room to tie the acts together, so to speak. I don't know if any of that makes sense, but really, that's how you think.

"And then we got to that title and it was incredible. It hit us like gangbusters how it really did work. You know, 'When the river was deep, I didn't falter.' Actually we had *worry. Falter* came later. *Worry* just laid there. *Falter* came from Simon.

"But you know what? The way that song came together is really neat. I feel that I've worked all my life to learn how to write that song in five minutes, because man, when it came, it came."

'Up Where We Belong' (theme song from the film *An Officer and a Gentleman)* by Buffy Sainte-Marie, Jack Nitzsche and Will Jennings, recorded by Joe Cocker and Jennifer Warnes.

Not only did the three songwriters never sit down together at any time to write this song, they never even communicated. In fact, two of the writers were *not* trying to write a song. They were unaware that there was a song in the works until it was developed and finished by the third writer.

This unusual circumstance came about when Will Jennings was called in to work on the film music in some unspecified fashion. The film had already been shot, and Jennings was given a rough-cut version that included a score – background music – by Sainte-Marie and Nitzsche. As Jennings recalled, "After I saw the rough cut of the film, I told Taylor Hackford [the director] that I thought I could hear a song just out of the bits and pieces. I heard a chorus here and a verse there and a release over here, and I had about half of it in my mind after I had finished the screening. I took the music out of the underscoring and put together the song. And then I wrote the lyric to it. Taylor had a couple of good suggestions on the lyrics – a couple of phrases that I changed – and that was basically it."

'Forty Hour Week' by Dave Loggins, Lisa Silver and Don Schlitz, recorded by Alabama.

Loggins wanted to co-write a song with the input of a fiddle, so he asked Lisa Silver, a session singer and violinist who had never written songs before, to collaborate. They came up with 'Maggie's Dream,' which later became a hit recorded by Don Williams.

"So we went on to 'Forty Hour Week,' " Loggins recalled. " 'Forty Hour Week' was a little thing I saw, a news clip, one morning on the Detroit auto workers. And I figured, for fun I'll just chat with them in the song. So we [he and Silver] were sitting in the office one day and we're writing this chorus, that's all we've got is the chorus. And we're having fun. We're sitting there fiddling away and playing, and I went, 'Hell, this sounds pretty good.' And all of a sudden I went, 'My God, I'm going to have to cover everybody that pulls a shift if we do this.' And by then I understood the need for someone that I felt was lyrically my equivalent or more, so I called Don in, asked him if he was doing anything. He said no. I got him into the tune, and he came in there spouting off these damn lyrics after I played the chorus, you know, just spoutin' 'em off. He said, 'I know how that goes: The guy that swings the hammer/Driving home the nails/The chick behind the counter/Ringing up the sales. You know what I'm talking about.'

"I said, 'Yeah, I do. Can you give me that one more time?' I started writing this down. I mean, right off the top of his head. If I'd said anything near that it would have taken me forever. And he does it in a pass.

"I think I said, 'It's for everyone that works behind the scene.' And this is my line, I know, 'With a spirit you can't replace with no machine.' Lisa's was a fiddle input more than anything. She was new at it. Her lyrical input wasn't a lot. It would probably be a lot more now because she's growing. Between us, Don and I probably split the lyrical content of 'Forty Hour Week.' I can't remember. I think it's because the lines are all right and good and up to both party's expectations that they just become both of you. That's interesting that I don't for the most part remember, except on those certain occasions, because you get blown away every once in a while."

'You've Got Your Troubles, I've Got Mine' by Roger Cook and Roger Greenaway, recorded by The Fortunes.

Greenaway had written a song (by himself) that Petula Clark recorded, called 'Everything in the Garden.' He wrote a different melody to the same chords and came up with the first two lines, 'I see that worried look upon your face/You've got your troubles, I've got mine.'

"That's all I had," he recalls. "So I played that to Cook and we sort of together got da da da . . . [the bridge melody]. And then it all took place in not more than an hour. Roger was going 'Wo-oh-oh . . . [singing wildly], so we had the whole song done. I was playing it through and he was dashing down lines, because he did most of that lyric. And within about 40 minutes, the whole thing, it was written the minute he was done. I was playing it down and singing away, and Cook said, 'You know what would be great? If we could have like a third melody. Just play it.' And I played it. I can remember just sitting there doing this . . . [playing the verse melody]. Already he had another melody going, which suddenly popped out at the end of the record. I don't remember anybody writing a melody like that − it was like a countermelody − and putting it as another piece in the song. It was almost too complicated. I think that was eventually the selling point of the song.''

They demoed the song and went on the road for some singing jobs. By the time they got back, their publishers had got the song cut by the then-unknown Fortunes. Greenaway said they had been hoping for The Supremes, so they were unhappy. By the time sales passed the two million mark, they had long since changed their minds.

'I'll Still Be Loving You' by Pam Rose, Mary Ann Kennedy, Todd Cerney and Pat Bunch, recorded by Restless Heart.

Rose and Kennedy scheduled a session with Cerney, who at that time was better known as a studio engineer than a writer. One reason they wanted to write with him, they explained, was that he had a lot of equipment – a Yamaha DX7 synthesiser, a drum machine and a sequencer – that at that time they did not have. "We just sat there with Todd and we started playing around," Rose said, "and I started playing these chords and the whole chord structure just sort of came out all at once. Todd was playing guitar. We hacked out a little of it, the form. And we'd talk about 'This sounds a little funny here, too this or too that.' I can't really remember.''

Then Kennedy began singing a melody on top of the chords and came up with the title. "As is the case with us lot, we'll start with the fade," Rose said. "Even though we had the melody pretty much from the get-go, a lot of times musically we'll start with the fade where you can stretch out, and then we focus back in, and I think that's when Mary Ann came up with the title.''

When it came to lyrics, Rose said, "We could have sat there for days." As Kennedy remembers, "Then we started to realise Todd wasn't any better at lyrics at that particular time, or at least on that song, than we were." Rose continued, "And we realised this feeling, this could be a classic love-through-the-ages love song. We just hung on to it.''

It did take, as Rose predicted, days – many of them. The song remained without lyrics for a year. Rose picked up the story, "Then we were listening to some tapes again and heard it and said, 'We've just got to have Pat write this.' And lo and behold, Pat called up one day and said, 'Hey, listen to this.' And there it was, just like that, almost to the word, the lyrics to that song.''

'Silver Bells' by Jay Livingston and Ray Evans, introduced by Bob Hope and Marilyn Maxwell in the film *The Lemon Drop Kid;* recorded by Bing Crosby.

Under contract to the film company, Livingston and Evans were given the assignment of writing a Christmas song for Hope and Maxwell to sing in the film, which was based on a Christmas story by Damon Runyon. The writers were nervous for several reasons, Livingston recalled. "We hadn't had a hit for a while and we had yearly options [on their publishing contracts] at this point, and we *knew* we couldn't write a hit Christmas song. There aren't any. You think about it. They're all old songs – 'Silent Night' through 'White Christmas.' We went up to the producers and we said, 'We don't want to write you a Christmas song because we'll never write you a hit song that way.' But the producers were adamant.

"So we were unhappy about it. We wrote a song called 'Tinkle Bell,' about the tinkly bells you hear at Christmas, Santa Claus and, since it took place in the city, the Salvation Army. And in order to make it different, we wrote it in three-quarter time because we couldn't think of a Christmas song in three-quarter time. And we also wrote the verse and the chorus so they could be played together at the same time, and that's the way the first record came out. It's a great sound. Nobody does it anymore. Bing Crosby's first record did that.

"Anyway, we wrote 'Tinkle Bell.' I went home and my wife said, 'What did you do?' I said, 'We wrote a song called "Tinkle Bell."' I played it for her. She said, 'You must be out of your mind.' She's a very strong critic. ' "Tinkle Bell?" *Tinkle's* got a bathroom meaning to it. People tinkle. You can't use that.'

"And that *was* a terrible title. So I went in to Ray and I said, 'We can't use that song.' He hates to rewrite, and he said, 'What's the matter with that?' I said, 'Tinkle has another meaning. We can't use a song about tinkling.' He said, 'Yeah, I guess you're right.'

"So we threw the whole song away, started to write a brand-new song, and we kept stealing from it. We stole part of the melody and part of the words. We said, 'That's a pretty song, you know?' So we took it finally and didn't change a word, except that we made it 'Silver Bells' instead of 'Tinkle Bell.' I had thought of 'Silver Bells,' but I was so careful. I thought, 'It sounds too much like "Jingle Bells," so let's keep it singular.' "

'Looking for Love' by Patti Ryan, Wanda Mallette and Bob Morrison, from the movie *Urban Cowboy*; recorded by Johnny Lee.

Morrison was the designated postbag listener at Combine Music in Nashville, screening the songs that hopeful writers sent in. Patti Ryan and Wanda Mallette had only the thinnest of connections to Morrison – Morrison knew Ryan's brother, and he had been on a high school track team with Mallette's husband – when they sent him 'Looking for Love.' Morrison believed it was *almost* a hit.

"The song lyrically was changed one line," he recalled. "There was a line in it that had 'debutantes' that we didn't feel – Johnny McRae [then vice-president of Combine] at first said, 'Gee that line just sounds like it's coming out of space or something.' So we changed that line to 'single bars.' The first chorus line was 'Looking for love in all the wrong places,' and then the second chorus line was changed. I felt like, if you're going to have the chord progression, why not repeat the second line against the different chord, because it just was wonderful when that second chord comes in and you're laying the same line ['Looking for Love'] – it was just a feel. I had to cut the bridge in half. And that's about it."

Incredibly, the song made it through a second postbag screening to get cut. "I couldn't get it cut in this town," Morrison said. "The publishing company here could not get that song cut in this town. It was turned down by 21 major acts. I sent it out to a friend in Hollywood, and he stuck it in a big bin for *Urban Cowboy*, and they somehow went through it – a bushel basket full of tapes – and picked it out."

'Somewhere in the Night' by Will Jennings and Richard Kerr, recorded by Helen Reddy, then Barry Manilow.

Kerr, an Englishman, met up with Texas-born, Nashville-trained Jennings in Los Angeles. They got together at the Sunset Marquis Hotel, where Kerr was staying. Jennings remembers possibly contributing something to the chorus music, but the melody is essentially Kerr's creation. Kerr also had a lyric – a very personal lyric about a new love. (He has said that he almost always has a lyric but it is almost never meaningful to anyone but himself.) Although this was their first effort together, it established a pattern of refusal of Kerr's lyrics. ''With Will, I don't think he's ever accepted anything that I've thrown at him lyrically,'' Kerr said in an interview. ''Because he'll come up with a better idea.'' That's exactly what Jennings did for 'Somewhere in the Night.'

'Why Not Me' by Harlan Howard, Sonny Throckmorton and Brent Maher, recorded by The Judds.

Maher, who produces The Judds, was nearing recording time for the mother-daughter act and he was short of material. He called Howard, who was reluctant for two reasons: 1) he was getting ready to take the summer off from songwriting (he can afford to); and 2) the majority of his many country hits had been written without the pressure of writing for a specific artist. He believed that was a hard way to write. ''That's gettin' in my way,'' he says. ''That's messin' up my song.''

Maher insisted and said he was coming over to Howard's house anyway, so Howard called in reinforcements in the person of Sonny Throckmorton. Even if Throckmorton had wanted to write 'on assignment' for The Judds, it wouldn't have helped. He had never heard of them. As Howard has described the scene, ''Sonny was hummin' and strummin'. After fighting over chords, they finally got this melody that sounded great, and Sonny was singing 'What about me . . . '.''

Throckmorton said the melody was based on one he'd had in his mind for a year or two. Howard looked to The Judds themselves for a story line. They have their roots in rural Kentucky, and the daughter, Wynona, was 19 years old at that time. From that inspiration, Howard developed the idea of a boy who has left a small town looking for big-time romance and the girl next door who tries to convince him that she is the answer.

'Nobody' by Dennis Morgan and Rhonda 'Kye' Fleming, recorded by Sylvia.

For about five years, Morgan and Fleming got together to write at the same time every day, Monday to Friday, whether they had an idea to work on or not. ''Right before we wrote 'Nobody,' '' Morgan recalls, ''there was about a three-week dry period. Nothing. It was hot down here in the South. Miserable weather. And we'd sit there day after day, and nothing happened. Tired, exhausted, but we didn't stop. We'd keep getting together.

''That's interesting because you get to the point where you get the giggles and everything is funny, then the pressure starts leaving, and for some strange reason it all starts flowing again. And lo and behold, we wrote 'Nobody' in about two hours – three weeks into that dry spell. And the next day we wrote 'Like Nothing Ever Happened' [another hit for Sylvia], and the next day we wrote another Number One, and I forget what it was. Three Number Ones in three days. You know, totally strange.''

'Give Her Thorns (And She'll Find the Roses)' by Dennis Linde and Bob Morrison, recorded by Michael Johnson as 'See the Love She Found in Me' and then by Gary Morris as 'The Love She Found in Me.'

Dennis Linde played Morrison a four-line chorus, which turned out to be the final version except for a lyric change in the second line. Morrison was reluctant at first to work on the song, feeling that he would be taking a free ride on an obvious hit idea. Morrison tells the story: "I said, 'Dennis, that's a hit chorus. Go back and do it. What do you need me for?'

"And he said, 'No, I've tried it for six months, Bob. I just can't find the melody that leads to this melody.'

"So I figured it would be pretty easy. Little did I know. I spent four months on it – I mean, you couldn't just put any melody going to that wonderful chorus melody. It had to be something that could at least stand in the same room with it. Otherwise you would have an unbalanced song. And so it took me a long time to get that little phrase that went right up into the melody smoothly.

"And then," Morrison continues, "I said, 'Hey, this is such a broad idea, it probably needs a bridge so you can repeat that chorus three times without boring everybody's ass off. So I wrote the bridge . . . Dennis and I got together three or four times over a three- or four-month period. I had to get the melody before we could go any farther."

'Mona Lisa' by Jay Livingston and Ray Evans, performed as an instrumental in the film *Captain Cary, USA*, recorded with lyrics by Nat King Cole.

"I wrote 'Mona Lisa' in the car," Livingston recalled. "It took me half an hour to drive in to the studio. We had to write an Italian song. It was a picture called *OSS*, which was the CIA during World War II. Alan Ladd was in a little Italian town, and they wanted some way of warning him that the Nazis were coming with a patrol. He was there with a little radio and the partisans, and they [the film company] said, 'Why doesn't somebody play a song on an accordion, a street guy.' He was blind but he could really see, and he'd start playing this song and that would warn Alan Ladd.

"I started to write something kind of scary, but we thought, 'No, that's going to warn the Germans.' So we wrote 'Mona Lisa.' How that was written was, Ray had the title 'Primadonna.' There was a big song called 'Ballerina' out. You shouldn't do it, but you do imitate . . . I was driving in the car, and I went 'Primadonna, primadonna, de da de da.' I wrote the whole melody. Of course, we didn't like 'Primadonna' as a song. He came up with the title 'Mona Lisa' the next day.

"Then they changed the title of the picture *OSS* to *After Midnight*. They said, 'We need a title song. Throw the lyric to "Mona Lisa" away and write "After Midnight," because that's a pretty melody and it sounds Italian.' So we wrote, 'I'm so lonely and it's only after midnight/Did we leave the candlelight, the wine too soon.' Same melody. We liked 'Mona Lisa.' We didn't think it was a hit, but it was pretty. But they wouldn't change it. They wanted that title song. They made a demo with a 44-piece Paramount orchestra of 'After Midnight,' which means that's the end of 'Mona Lisa.'

"Then we picked up *Variety* a month later and it said, 'Alan Ladd's new picture, *After Midnight,* is now called *Captain Cary, USA.* ' We said, 'Hell, let's go see if we can get our "Mona Lisa" lyric back.' So we went up to one of the executives and he said, 'We don't have a demo.' I said, 'Yes, you do.' See, what I did was, there was half an hour left on the recording date, and I said to this guy, 'Would you just sing the same melody and read these words off, just for me?' I don't know why I did it – just for protection."

The demo was retrieved and played for Nat King Cole, who put the song on the B-side of 'The Greatest Inventor of Them All,' a religious song. Livingston and Evans, meanwhile, went on a two-week promotional junket with Paramount, and when they had any spare time, they called on deejays, encouraging them to turn the record over. By the time the trip was over, 'Mona Lisa' was a hit.

CHAPTER ELEVEN

SCHEDULING

From all the examples in the previous chapters, surely some keys, some secrets to collaboration, should emerge. Unfortunately, the songwriters themselves don't really have the key, and you may go crazy trying to figure it out. As Cynthia Weil has said, "Everybody has their own little procedures they go through and can tell you their little tricks. I would have times when I'd listen to a certain writer until that turned me off. Or I'd listen to the radio, don't listen to the radio, wear my shoes, don't wear my shoes, write in the living room, write in the den. And it never comes the same way twice, and that's why I think we're all a little nuts."

The methods described in the examples do vary widely. Dennis Morgan and Rhonda Fleming had a standing appointment every morning, Monday to Friday for five years, ideas or no ideas. Roger Cook and Roger Greenaway, on the other hand, got together to write only when one of them had a well-developed idea to run with. Pam Rose, Mary Ann Kennedy and Pat Bunch work mostly over the phone and hardly ever get together face to face.

That covers the extremes, but that's only for *regular* writing teams. Even more variations (even among those same writers) crop up when you consider writers who work with more than one partner. When Greenaway visits Nashville or Morgan visits London or Los Angeles for a two- or three-week writing trip, their daily schedules are full, sometimes with a different co-writer every day or two. Dave Loggins, on the other hand, usually blocks out a one-week segment to work with a co-writer. Greenaway, Morgan and Loggins write head to head. In contrast, Will Jennings works when there is a project to work on, and he works alone, often writing lyrics to a melody without even a title to start from. Bob Morrison writes melodies to lyrics, or in other ways doctors songs, with pen-pal collaborators, some of whom he's never met.

So where is the pattern? Where is the common ground? "Things would just fly in all over the place all the time because it was such a creative atmosphere," Dennis Morgan said. Dave Loggins talked about "a chemistry – a oneness" and the "positive energy . . . Whether you had an idea or a piece of something or you had nothing, it was going to happen." The common ground is their excitement when they talk about collaboration at its highest level. If it doesn't come through here in print, I assure you the edge was there in their voices in the interviews. They sounded like gamblers on a roll.

Creativity was at its highest point in many of these accounts, but how did it get there? The most common conditions to inspire and exploit creativity are an office and an appointment schedule – two rather cold, disciplinary sort of considerations that seem to represent yet another intrusion of business into art. But they are as important to success as any other aspect of collaboration.

With scheduling, the required business skill is organisation. Unfortunately for the songwriter, the average salesman has a much easier time efficiently scheduling his sales calls than the writer has scheduling co-writing sessions for maximum productivity. The reason for this, which should be familiar to you by now, is that every co-writing relationship is different. The key, as always, is to go with what works best for you *and* – here's where it gets complicated – for your co-writer *and* for your partnership.

Spontaneity

Not all co-written hits started as a notation in an appointment book, of course. Dean Dillon was having breakfast with Shel Silverstein at the Third Coast restaurant in Nashville (also known as 'The Rock and Roll Hotel'), when he saw his friend Frank Dycus at another table drinking a beer. Dillon walked over, mentioned his new record deal with RCA, and as he described it, 'tortured' Dycus into writing with him – right there at the table. Dillon sat down and voiced an idea about being wrapped around a woman's finger and getting unwound tonight. Dycus reversed the situation, suggesting that the woman had been wrapped around the man's finger but has just broken free, and the team wrote the George Strait hit 'Unwound.'

Another example. After a Carpenters concert in Nashville, Richard Carpenter invited his long-time friend and collaborator John Bettis to take a ride in the Lear jet the group was travelling in. Inspired by the view from the air, they wrote the Carpenters' hit 'Top of the World' on the flight.

And another. Willie Nelson and Waylon Jennings wrote 'Good Hearted Woman' during a poker game. Nelson's wife, Connie, wrote down the lyrics. Willie and Waylon didn't miss a hand.

Nickolas Ashford believes in spontaneity, and he has evidence to support it. After he and his wife, Valerie Simpson, spent a fruitless day at the office trying to write, they knocked off and headed for happy hour. In the taxi on the way to the bar, with their friend Joshie Armstrong, they dashed off 'Let's Go Get Stoned' in about 10 minutes. (*Stoned* in those days still referred to drinking.) "You can't schedule your creativity," Ashford says. But his faith in spontaneity is tempered by his wife and partner, who says they pull each other out of creative slumps and spark each other's creative moods.

There's something to be said for spontaneity in songwriting: don't deny it. Livingston and Evans were once watching composer Victor Young conduct a film soundtrack session when the director, Cecil B. de Mille, rejected a piece of the music. It was 'Swing Low, Sweet Chariot,' and a group of blacks were singing it as they rowed across a river. Young told the 44-piece orchestra and the 12 singers to take a 10 minute break, and he motioned to Livingston and Evans to come with him. As they were walking upstairs to an office, Livingston asked what the scene was about. Young replied, "They're rowing home." They had 'Rowing Home' written and ready to record by the time the break was over. So don't refuse a sudden inspiration or invitation just because you're not in your songwriting office or your co-writer didn't have an appointment.

When

Songs do occasionally drop out of the sky into your lap, but you won't get far as a professional if your songwriting technique is to sit around and wait for them.

Most professional songwriters work like the majority or working people – in the daytime. They wake up and go to work. Most start at a reasonable hour, say 10 a.m., when they've had time enough and caffeine enough to wake up, and when their minds are still fresh and clear – before their thoughts can be diverted by business or other non-writing concerns. I say *they* when I should say *I*; this is the way I work best. I find it difficult to change my train of thought effectively in the middle of the day. If I spend a morning making phone calls, copying tapes and pitching songs, I find it hard to switch to a writing frame of mind in the afternoon. And if a morning writing session has been productive, I find that that song – especially if it's unfinished – is the dominant thought in my mind, making it hard to switch from one writer in the morning to another in the afternoon. If a morning session has been unproductive, I'm not in a good mood for writing or anything else.

One advantage of a daily schedule is the discipline it imposes on a writer. "Songwriters are scattered," Dave Loggins explained. "The good ones, they're really scattered and have massive inconsistencies, and one thing that keeps them, and myself included, scheduled and regimented more is being here to work with somebody at nine-thirty or ten o'clock, because you are responsible to the other party, as they are to you. I mean, hell, you can tell yourself to sleep on, you'll get to it. But when someone's waiting, you're more scheduled."

Other writers work differently. Some work fast enough that they routinely finish a song in two or three hours or they prefer to let it sit if they can't finish it quickly, and they think nothing of scheduling a morning session with one writer and an afternoon with another. To them the change of pace is preferable to hammering away on one song all day.

The situation is different if you started a song at a previous session and either you or your co-writer has finished it alone. If you are reasonably sure the song is in fact finished, then a clear mind and a ready-to-work attitude is not so necessary. The purpose of your appointment is more-like a meeting to approve a final plan rather than to devise a new one.

Of course, not every songwriter has the luxury of making a living as a songwriter. Even writers whose names appear with some regularity in the record charts may still make most of their money as musicians, engineers or producers. Like anyone else with a day job, they can't schedule co-writing sessions every morning. They have to work their songwriting efforts around their jobs.

For many aspiring writers, particularly those whose jobs are not music-related, this means writing at night and at weekends. This also means it will be harder to find co-writers, especially if you're trying to work with full-time songwriters. After a day at work writing songs, a full-time songwriter is no different from anybody else. He'd rather go home to his family or go out for some entertainment than extend his working day another three or four hours. If your usual habit is to down a couple of drinks after work, then it's going to be difficult to go back to work. However, if you're going to be successful as a songwriter, you have to give it a high priority in your life. If you want to write with a certain writer who is available only at night, then you should be dedicated enough to make the proper adjustments in your personal habits.

Some songs get written very late at night. In 'She Believes in Me' Steve Gibbs describes the classic scene in which the writer comes home late and gets side-tracked on his way to bed by his guitar (his piano in the original version) and a song idea. In real life, Roger Cook and Bobby Wood "just kind of got started singing at three in the morning," Cook said, in describing how they wrote 'Talking in Your Sleep'.

In the seventies, when amphetamines were more powerful, more readily available, and the most popular drug among musicians and songwriters, I'm sure a lot more songs were written in the early morning hours. I'm also reasonably sure that the overwhelming majority of late-night songwriting sessions are spontaneous, an out-growth of dinner or drinks together or some other activity earlier in the evening. Unless you and your co-writer are both on a schedule that has you awake with free time at 3.00 a.m., don't expect much from *scheduled* co-writing sessions at that hour.

How Long

How much time should you set aside for a writing session? It depends on your attention span. You want to give it two or three hours at the very least. Dennis Morgan prefers to clear out the whole day. Most of the sessions in a publishing office go for a couple of hours in the morning until you get stuck or hungry or both. If the song is taking shape, usually there will be a productive period after lunch. If not, lunch could extend into happy hour and the song set aside to be finished at a later date.

The one thing you don't want to do is have to stop in the middle of writing because you scheduled something else and didn't give yourself enough time. Leave yourself some openings in your schedule; an open schedule will be easier to adjust than a tight one.

How Often

Professional writers are basically working stiffs – they work every day. But that doesn't necessarily mean they fill every day with co-writing appointments. The key is to adjust your schedule for maximum efficiency, and that means for quality as well as quantity. If you're scheduling morning and afternoon writing sessions Monday to Friday, you may be turning out 10 songs a week. But unless they are 10 *good* songs, you need to cut your schedule back and spend more time on each song. Or it may be that you can't finish all those songs, in which case you need to cut back temporarily in order to clean house.

Too sparse scheduling can be a problem, too. If you schedule only one writer on Monday and a different one on Thursday, the following could happen. You almost finish a song on Monday. You *do* finish it yourself on Tuesday. You've got a great idea that evolved from that Monday session that you want to work on with your Monday writer, but it's only Wednesday, and you won't see him until next Monday. That idea is burning up your brain but you have to put it on hold and concentrate on your Thursday session with a different writer. You obviously need to adust your schedule. Schedule two days or more in a row with your Monday writer – whatever it takes. Cancel Thursday if you really think you have to (but don't wait until Thursday morning to do it).

What may be happening with this Monday co-writer is that you and he are suddenly on a roll. The relationship, to use Dennis Morgan's term, 'clicks.' One idea leads to another, and you are writing better and better songs as fast as you can put the words down on the paper. If that's happening, don't wait until Monday if you can get together tomorrow.

I said that songwriters work every day, but I should add, 'when they're working.' Some writers work hard for a while and then take off for a while. A writer who works mostly on projects, as Will Jennings does, is going to have a schedule with weeks at a time blocked out – some for intensive work and some for rest and recuperation between projects. Others work day to day, but then, as Harlan Howard was about to do when he got the call to write 'Why Not Me,' they may take the entire summer off.

You may not be able to afford to take a summer off. If you're trying hard to establish yourself as a songwriter, you may believe that you really can't afford to take even a week off. But if the quality of your writing starts falling off a bit, if you don't seem to be getting any fresh ideas, you may not be able to afford *not* to take a break.

Where

Like any other businessman, you need a songwriting office, a place set up for work, a place that puts you in the mood for work when you are there. Whether it's a 6x6 cubicle in an office building, a corner of your living room, a seaside chalet or a hut in the woods, seclusion from the day-to-day is common to most songwriters' work habits. If you live alone, your entire house or flat may function as your office, your writing place.

The one notable exception is cars. For some reason, a lot of songs are written in cars. Boudleaux Bryant recalled the beginnings of 'Bye Bye Love,' saying that while he and his wife, Felice, were driving from their old house to a new one, the phrase 'bye bye love' "just dropped into my mind" complete with melody. Sammy Fain wrote the music to 'Dear Hearts and Gentle People' while driving to the race track. Sammy Cahn and Jule Styne were on their way to the beach when they wrote 'Let It Snow, Let It Snow, Let It Snow.' Dave Loggins came up with the chorus of 'Everyday' on the 20-minute drive from his home to his publishing office. The melodies to 'Mona Lisa' and 'To Each His Own' are two of many pieces of work Jay Livingston accomplished on his daily 30-minute drive to the office. Johnny Mercer and Harold Arlen worked out 'Ac-cent-chu-ate the Positive' in a car.

The reason for this kind of creative production is not hard to comprehend. A moving car gives you isolation from outside contact (cellular phones notwithstanding) and the diversion of changing scenery, while the challenge of arriving alive keeps the mind alert. I'm not suggesting that you call a collaborator and say, "Let's get together at ten tomorrow. We'll drive to Memphis and see what we come up with." (That is an interesting possibility, however. If you *do* do that, let me know how it comes out.) What I am suggesting, as I have suggested in every aspect of collaboration, is to find the way that works best.

CHAPTER TWELVE

CRITICISING AND EVALUATING

You and your co-writer have finished a song, or at least you have a complete song written. It has music and lyrics that go together, and it's an acceptable song form. Okay, you have *a* song. What you want to know is whether or not it's a *good* song, whether someone is going to like it and cut it and make you some money. How do you get an accurate evaluation?

One of the advantages of collaboration set forth in the opening chapter is the instant criticism you get from your partner. Even if you did not write the entire song face to face, but did large portions separately, you and your partner should still have maintained some contact and communication during the writing process, and thus gained each other's critical assessments as you went along. It's likely that at many points along the way, one of you played portions of the song while the other tried to listen and evaluate with a more objective perspective.

Now it's time for you both to try to forget for a moment that it's your baby. Forget you've ever heard the song before, and try to listen to it as if you were a publisher or an artist hearing it for the first time. Don't play it live. Put it on tape, and play it back. You know what you wanted to write; did you fulfil the plan? Does it work? Can you hear an artist singing it?

Agreeing

You probably realise you should ask these questions whether you collaborate or write alone. The difference between this list and the others is the addition of the question 'Do you both agree?' Writing alone, you don't have to have anyone's blessing to proceed from this point. Even if everyone from spouse to publisher dislikes the song, if you believe in it, you can push it. If you have a partner who believes the song is not there yet, you can still proceed without him, but you're asking for trouble.

Together you have to answer the question, 'What have we got?' (The answer you're looking for is, 'A *cuttable* song.') You'd think that if two people worked together on a song from beginning to end, they would be in agreement over the finished product. And if you were communicating with your partner as you were writing, you probably do agree, whether the assessment is favourable or unfavourable. A weak line or an awkward chord change in an otherwise good song will probably not cause any major disagreements – those are relatively easy to identify and fix. And even if the whole song is weak, if the idea is not exploited properly or simply not good enough, that shouldn't be too hard for you and your partner to see, either.

So far, so good. But what if you agree that the song is not right, but you disagree on what to do about it? You think it's written as well as it can be written, but *you* think now that the idea is only average and therefore the song is destined to be average. You want to shelve it and move on. Your partner thinks it's salvageable, although he's not sure yet what direction it ought to take.

What if you write a song that is neither fish nor fowl? It has a strong idea and is well written except for one problem. It has country-dialect lyrics and jazz-funk music. You and your partner love it like it is, but you also both realise that to get it cut, it needs to be one style or the other. But which one? It sounds country when you sing it and funky when he does.

As you can see, evaluating a song – trying to figure out exactly what it is you've written – is not always a simple task. And I can't give you the answers. You and your partner will have to find them yourselves.

Collaborator-Critics

One evaluation problem peculiar to collaboration may come into play if certain portions of the song or certain writing responsibilities were clearly separated.

To illustrate, let's say one writer wrote all the lyrics, the other all the music. When the song is finished and the tape played back, the composer says, "That third line of the chorus could be stronger, don't you think?" And the lyricist says, "I think it says what we want to say. It's the melody that's the problem. To me, it doesn't seem to go anywhere at that point."

These writers have made these criticisms with all due respect for each other, and they haven't taken offence at the tone of each other's criticism. The problem is that the *lyric* specialist is offering his services as an expert on *music*, and vice versa. Each is invading the other's area of expertise.

Pam Rose, Mary Ann Kennedy and Pat Bunch have an accepted area of responsibility in their writing, and they often find themselves in that situation. They have no set way of dealing with it except to rely on their respect for one another's talents. For example, Rose and Kennedy, who write the music, are very picky about Bunch's lyrics. Their demand that the lyric be 'singable' for them sometimes results in a lot of hard and tedious work for Bunch. Other times, however, they will trust the person who is the team's 'expert' in the area in question. "I'm sure sometimes Pat's not totally blown away with the music," Kennedy said, "but she'll go, 'Mary Ann knows' or 'Pam knows.' And even though 90 percent of the time I won't be totally blown away with Pat's lyrics, I'll live with it and I'll realise why it's great. Maybe I'm not particularly into it at the time, but I know that Pat is so great."

What we're getting into here is a debate over the role of the critic that goes back to Sophocles' time, a debate that is perpetuated every time a record gets a bad review and the artist says to the critic, "I'd like to see *you* make a record." Is a critical opinion valid if the critic has no special talent himself in the field he's criticising? Does a lyricist have any business telling a composer how to write melodies? The answer is ultimately yes, but the issue is more complicated than yes or no.

Let's say you're a lyricist and you're working with Richard Rodgers. He criticises your lyrics, and you think (but out of respect, you don't say it) "Stick to melodies, old-timer. I'm the lyricist and I know what I'm doing." Rodgers may not have written too many lyrics, but he's worked with two of the greatest lyricists of all time, and you can bet he knows when your work doesn't measure up to Hammerstein's or Hart's. So shelve your ego and get back to work.

Creative Differences

But wait. There's a more serious problem here, as I tried to indicate by putting *old-timer* in your thoughts. What if one of Rodgers's points of criticism is that you rhymed *send* with *again* or *past* with *hats*. To him, that is unforgivably sloppy. To you, it's no big deal because people just don't put that much importance on perfect rhymes anymore, not like they did in the thirties and forties. In this song, what the lyric says is much more important than how perfectly it rhymes. Forget egos – what you have here is a *creative difference.*

A creative difference can be more subtle than that. If part of your writing philosophy is to widen the boundaries of country music by incorporating unusual chords and chord progressions into your songs, and your partner is just as intent on furthering country music by writing better melodies *within* the traditional three- or four-chord structures, you have a creative difference, a philosophical difference. It may be as deeply ingrained as a personality trait and never be put to rest. If all goes well, though, it can be resolved for the sake of a song.

You *do* want to resolve any creative differences. Otherwise you've wasted a song idea as well as the time it took to write it. As in any other type of conflict, an arbitrator might be helpful.

If you have a publisher (whether you're actually on staff or not), you might as well go to him, because you're going to have to play the song for him sooner or later. You may want to fill him in on the problem beforehand, or you may just want to let him listen cold so you can get an unbiased opinion. Most successful publishers got that way in part because they are good at evaluating songs and working with songwriters. Their evaluations and suggestions are worth listening to, because after all, they are the ones whose job it is to pitch the songs. If they don't know anything else, at least they know what kind of songs they can get cut.

For that same reason, you may *not* want a publisher's evaluation. You may feel that a publisher's ears are programmed along narrow concepts – not just what is or isn't a hit or a cuttable song, but again, what *he* can get cut – and that those ears are also weary and jaded from hours upon hours of listening to songs. You believe you will get a more useful assessment from a fellow songwriter, or an engineer, or anyone who can give you an informed opinion. That's what Yip Harburg and Harold Arlen did when Harburg thought Arlen's melody for 'Somewhere Over the Rainbow' was wrong for Judy Garland. He thought it sounded too grandiose, that it was better suited for someone like Nelson Eddy than a 16-year-old girl. In an effort to resolve the issue, they played it to Ira Gershwin, who suggested keeping the melody but picking up the tempo and simplifying the arrangement.

However, a professional musical ear is not always the best judge of a song's hit potential. You may want an outside opinion that is unbiased by music-business influences and unjaded from hearing songs all day long – someone who listens to music for pleasure and not for a living. Spouses, especially non-musical spouses, have traditionally been brutally honest critics (remember, had it not been for Jay Livingston's wife, we might be singing 'Tinkle Bell' instead of 'Silver Bells' at Christmas time). If your child starts singing your song around the house, that's an encouraging sign. One producer I know – and this is no lie – tries out his possible singles on his dog, who howls when he hears a hit.

By now, a new problem has come up – evaluating the evaluator. How much credibility do you give to the independent finding of the third party, especially if that finding runs counter to your position? If you and your partner can agree beforehand to abide by the arbitrator's decision, that will make things easier. Ultimately, you have to weigh all the opinions – especially your partner's – against your own opinions and principles and then do what you think is best for you.

My advice is to do whatever it takes to work out a compromise. If you have to alternate authority – my way on this song, your way on the next; or better, my way on my *ideas*, your way on yours – that's one way. Whatever you do, you lose if you can't work something out.

If you like your song, your co-writer likes your song, your publisher likes it, an artist likes it, and record buyers like it, then you have no problems. If you have disagreements that you can't resolve, you only have one problem – finding a new collaborator. If, however, you and your co-writer have agreed in evaluating your song that something needs to be changed, you have the dreaded task of rewriting ahead of you.

CHAPTER THIRTEEN

REWRITING

Show me a songwriter who likes to rewrite and I'll show you someone who enjoys going to the dentist. There is no greater feeling than to have finished a song, and there is no worse feeling than to discover then that you haven't after all.

Everybody hates to rewrite. In Jay Livingston's story of 'Silver Bells,' when he got to the part where he told his partner a rewrite was necessary, Livingston grimaced and groaned to convey Ray Evans's reaction. More important, though, is the fact that Evans's protest was nominal. He knew it, too. What Livingston, Evans and all professional songwriters know is that, like dental work, when a rewrite has to be done, it has to be done. It comes with the job.

Why is it so hard? Because you're probably already into a great new idea and you don't want to stop your forward momentum and backtrack into an old idea. And because to rewrite effectively, you are often faced with the difficult mental task of erasing old thought-patterns and etching new ones into your mind in order to get a new idea or direction.

The pros do it, and from looking at their stories, there is no shortcut. The only way to make rewriting easier is to call it something else – like *fixing* or *finishing*. Alan Jay Lerner had a tough time with the lyric to 'On a Clear Day You Can See Forever.' He spent two weeks of what he called "the usual run-of-the-mill torture" and then set aside the first three hours of every morning to work on that song. Eight months later, when he finally finished it, he had written 91 complete lyrics. That's 90 rewrites, although he never called them that because to him the song was never finished until the ninety-first.

Dennis Morgan said the Ronnie Milsap hit 'Smoky Mountain Rain' is a combination and evolution of four different songs he and Rhonda Fleming wrote over a period of three weeks. "Those titles are gone now," Morgan said. "I can't even remember what they were. At one time it was 'Appalachian Rain.' Another time it was another 'Rain' title, with two or three of these little elements in it. Another time we stripped it down completely, ended up coming up with that final melody with a completely different idea. And what we eventually did, we didn't necessarily take from each song. They were stepping stones that ended up becoming the same story – only a little stronger each time."

Another example: although the lyrics to the TV theme for *Bonanza* were sung only once – in the pilot – Livingston and Evans have written two additional versions. Even though the series is in reruns all over the world, and the theme is the most lucrative copyright in their considerable catalogue, they are still not satisfied with the lyrics.

If you haven't already figured out the key to rewriting from the examples, Morgan lays it out for you: "It's not giving up when you know that there's a germ of a song there somewhere, and then it's a matter of refining it down to something you know is right."

These writers' personal standards of perfection won't allow a song to rest until it is right. That demand for perfection – John Bettis mentioned it when he said he looks for a co-writer who "won't settle" – is the one quality, I believe, that sets the successful songwriters apart from the rest. It may be even more important than talent and inspiration. That quality is best put to use in rewriting.

All of this applies whether you write alone or with a partner. Like everything else, it just gets more complicated when you have a partner. It sometimes seems easier just to forget the song and try to do better on the next one. You can do that if you're writing alone, but when there is a co-writer involved, you would be reneging on your responsibility to give it your best effort. Again, think of it as finishing. You wouldn't stop writing a song halfway through and let your co-writer finish it. If you need to rewrite, then you're simply not finished yet.

When Co-writers Agree

The basic rule is to rewrite when your song needs it. But with collaboration, you hope that the applicable rule is to rewrite because you and your partner agree that your song needs it. Ideally, you listen to the song you have just written together, and you recognise *together* the parts that need fixing. No problem. Even if it's the whole song that needs fixing – the title's good but the song is just boring – you may not agree or even know where you went wrong or what to do to fix it, but at least you agree that something has to be done.

At Publisher's Request

You play the song for your publisher – not to get his evaluation, but because you believe it is finished. Your publisher agrees – except for two lines that bother him. You and your partner gang up on him and convince him he's wrong, but you may have won a hollow victory. If those two lines bother your publisher now, they will probably bother him every time he hears your song, and he may not pitch it as often because of that. Regardless of the artistic merits of the lines in question, it's probably time for a rewrite.

If you know your publisher, you may have already rewritten. A co-writer and I once had a line in the middle of a fairly light-hearted song that would stop you cold. It wasn't out of metre and it made sense within the context of the song, but it also had a world of other, more serious meanings. I loved it. My co-writer, even though he was the one who came up with it, wasn't so sure. He *was* sure the line would never get past our publisher. I knew he was probably right, so we had the alternate line ready when our publisher – as predicted – said, "That line bothers me."

At Artist's or Producer's Request

Your song may go farther down the line before you get a rewrite request. You, your co-writer and your publisher all like it; you demo it, and a producer likes it but feels the third verse needs to say something else. It may or may not be time for a rewrite. You and your partner have to consider how important the cut is versus how important the song is to you as it stands. Is this a major artist? Is this a major change in the song? Do you need the money now or can you afford to wait for another cut? Do you have enough confidence in the song that you believe another artist will cut it? Harlan Howard and Bobby Braddock did, after George Jones's producer asked them to take *crayons* out of 'I Don't Remember Loving You.' The song was written from the viewpoint of a mental patient being visited by a former lover, and in one line, the man reveals his mental condition quite clearly by asking the woman to hand him his crayons. Howard and Braddock happened to be fond of that particular line, and their response to the rewrite request was, as Howard put it, "That line stays. We'll get somebody else to cut a hit on it." And they did – John Conlee.

But that was one song and one set of circumstances. In a similar situation with almost the same cast of characters, Braddock and Curly Putman rewrote 'He Stopped Loving Her Today' several times to get their George Jones cut. Why the opposite reactions to rewriting? Obviously, in the first case, the writers felt strongly that the song was right just the way it was, and in the second case they knew themselves that it wasn't. There's no set way to deal with this situation other than to be sure to take all the factors into consideration before making your decision.

Lack of Interest Everybody in town has turned down your song. You still believe in it, and you reassure yourself by trying to remember all the great songs that were rejected many times before they were finally cut. Nevertheless, your confidence is developing a few small cracks. Discuss the possibility of a rewrite with your co-writer. If he's still a true believer in the song, keep plugging it. But if he's having doubts about it too, take another look at it. Re-evaluate it. If you've done everything you can to try to get it cut, maybe a rewrite is in order.

One Writer Only One of the more frustrating rewriting situations arises when one writer wants to rewrite and his partner does not. This predicament is especially trying if you are the one who had the idea – and it was a great one – but the song you wrote didn't do it justice. Since it was your idea, it probably means more to you than to your co-writer. You still believe in it; he's ready to move on to something new. Unfortunately you are on your own now. You have to prove to your partner that the song can be written better before he'll change his mind. *Saying* that it needs to be rewritten is not enough to convince him. You have to *show* him. You have to come up with some new lines or new music on your own.

You may want to call in a third co-writer to help you fix the song, or you may wish you could just take the idea back and start all over again with a different co-writer. Most collaborators would not object to the first option *if* they thought the song was dead – a third of something being better than half of nothing. The second option, however, is asking for trouble. Unless it's a case of a complete separation of melody and lyric, a case in which you wrote one part and are rejecting your co-writer's part, you can't just take back an idea, shake off the song that was written around it, and act like it's new again. It's like a judge telling a jury to disregard a remark. Thoughts are not erasable. If you do call in a third writer, make sure your original co-writer knows what you're doing, and try to persuade him to agree. He'll probably change his mind about the song if the rewrite begins to look promising.

We've assumed that your co-writer doesn't want to rewrite because he thinks the song is not salvageable. But it may be that he thinks it is finished. Now you're the one who is going to be the source of irritation. While your co-writer is trying to set up a demo session, you keep coming at him with new ideas for the song. Even after the demo session, after the song is being pitched, you keep after him. His response to your suggestions has become automatic: ''The song is stronger like it is. Leave it alone.'' He believes in it. He's trying to get it cut. What is your problem?

Why are you doing this? Probably because the song didn't end up the way you envisioned it. Again, you are on your own in rewriting it. It is probably not a good idea to call in a third writer at this late stage. Don't give up if you're not satisfied with your song, but don't make life miserable for your co-writer with a constant assault of rewrite ideas. If you are right, then the song probably won't get cut as it is and your co-writer may eventually come around to your opinion without any further prodding. If and when you do find something better, get it into shape and make the strongest, most polished presentation you can to your co-writer.

Solicited Rewrites

Finally, you and your partner agree on the need for a rewrite. If the changes needed are major – if, for example, the idea is good but the song isn't – you may want to call in a song doctor. What you'll get is a new perspective as well as someone to do some or all of the rewriting for you. What you'll have to give up is another share of the credit and possibly the song itself. Dennis Morgan was not happy with John Schweers's rewrite of 'It's Another I-Love-You Day.' Schweers made it 'It's Another I-Love-You Kind of Day' so it would phrase better, and he replaced Morgan's wordy verses with something simpler. Schweers predicted Charley Pride would cut it, and Morgan recalls, ''I thought, 'No way. This is a weak song.' '' (Morgan changed his mind when he got the Pride cut.)

Unsolicited Rewrites

Sometimes your song gets rewritten without you, without your knowledge. If your rewriter is a publisher or a writer called in by a publisher, he is probably acting in good faith, trying to fix your song so he can get it cut. Still, you have every right – including legal – to object. If it's a producer or an artist, he may also be trying to fix it in order to cut it, but the situation is complicated by the possibility of the cut – is the cut worth the price? The price may be a percentage of the song or simply a different song from the one you wrote. Legally, of course, the song is yours and you don't have to cut anybody else in, even if – as in the 'Hound Dog' example in Chapter 5 – the new version is the one recorded.

In the latter case, you (your publisher, actually) also have one further legal recourse – to refuse to grant a licence for the release of the record. Your legal rights are clear, but your proper course of action is not. Looking again at the 'Hound Dog' case, you may just want to protect your rights, rather than actually stopping the release of the record. It may well be worthwhile to give the unsolicited co-writer a piece of the song if the contribution and the cut are significant. Take all the factors into consideration and decide. And don't wait to make your decision until the record is released and the extra writer's name is already printed on the label.

Scheduling Rewrites

If you have major work to do on a song, you can make an appointment the same way you would for a regular co-writing session. Usually, rewriting sessions like that are more for clean-up purposes – for knocking a song into shape or making sure the writers are in agreement over which is the final version. Among collaborators who do not have standing appointments, I would say the biggest part of rewriting is done independently. You play a song for a song doctor, or just hand him a tape, and say, "See if you can do anything with this." He takes it home and calls you later. You probably don't get together until he's actually done some work.

The same thing happens with your original partner. Once you know what the song needs, it's "I'll call you when I've got something." To illustrate: Jimbeau Hinson and I wrote a song originally called something like 'When She Leaves, the Lady Leaves With Me.' Contained in the chorus was the phrase 'liquored lies.' The moment he came up with those words, Jimbeau said that should be our title, but we finished the song as we had started it. Our publisher heard it that same afternoon and was not knocked out by it, so we immediately decided to start again from "Liquored Lies." We did not set an appointment; we only agreed to try to develop the idea independently and call when one of us had something. The call came from Jimbeau the very next morning at 6.30 a.m. I wasn't surprised by the hour. I was lying in bed, half-awake already, thinking about a new melody for the song. Jimbeau had the whole thing written except for one nagging little lyric problem. While we were taking care of business at our publishing office that afternoon, we filled up four or five pages of a notepad with possible lines, and we finally found the right ones. We never did set up a rewriting appointment.

Avoiding Rewrites

There is a way to avoid rewriting, but it is just as hard as rewriting, and that is to do it right the first time. It sounds flippant, but it's true. You can see a thorough method in use in the writers' workshop session in Chapter 8, when Don Pfrimmer goes to great lengths to get the concept of the song straight in his mind. He wants to be sure they're all working on the same idea, of course, but he also doesn't want to finish the song and then look at it and decide it should have been written a different way. In other words, he doesn't want to have to rewrite. Once again, that desire for perfection asserts itself. If you keep thoroughness in mind throughout the writing of a song, you may have a harder time finishing the song, but you will lessen the chances of having to rewrite it.

CHAPTER FOURTEEN

PUBLISHING

You and your collaborator *did* give each other an idea, before you started writing, of what you planned to do with your publishing, didn't you? If you have already taken into consideration some of the possible situations and problems, you're ahead of the game. If you haven't, you have to now. Now that you have a song written, you have to deal specifically with publishing issues and make some of your most important business decisions.

The demo is the single most important concern outside of writing the song, and now it is the most immediate. You must have a demo to pitch a song, whether that demo is a home-made work tape or a 24-track production. The cost of a suitable demo (which depends on the type of song, of course) is one of the prime factors in determining what you should do with your publishing. You also need to consider how active and effective a prospective publisher is. An active, pitching publisher is a luxury. If you have a demo, you can pitch the song yourself, whether your publisher does or not.

If you *can* afford a demo, you may want to hold on to your publishing, for the time being, at least. If you *can't* afford a demo, you can't afford to be your own publisher – it's as simple as that. (Well, actually, it's never as simple as that.) Here are some of the publishing configurations and situations you may run into with two writers on a song.

Both are Staff If you are both staff writers, you have no paperwork to worry about, even if you write for different companies. That's the publisher's business reponsibility. And you have no problems if both publishers are in agreement, whether they like the song or hate the song. If they are in disagreement, then you and your co-writer have to start playing politics in order to get it demoed. Just as you would if you had written the song alone, go to the publisher who has the strongest positive feeling and lobby for the song on that publisher's demo session. In most co-publishing situations, both publishers do not co-produce the demo sessions. More than likely, one will produce and pay for the session and then prorate the costs and bill the co-publisher. (Because of abuses of that method, some publishers have included in their co-publishing agreements a limit on demo cost liability without prior approval.) Using this method, you are in a sense working behind the back of one of the publishers, gambling that when the demo is done, he will change his mind about the song. So be sure the song is worth that gamble.

There may be times when you have to work behind both publishers' backs to get your song demoed. If you are at the point where your publisher is not looking over your shoulder at demo sessions, there is a way to do this, and that is to slip it in on a session. You or your collaborator gets approval on four songs (or whatever the publisher thinks is a reasonable number) for a demo session. You plan ahead and work efficiently so that you have time to do five songs. I shouldn't have to tell you which is the fifth song. You tell the publisher, "Well, we were left with 15 minutes at the end of the session, so we just tossed it out there to the musicians." You point out that he got five songs for the price of four.

A strong word of caution: you had better believe in this song and be willing to fight for it, because you are risking your relationship with your publisher. Your publisher may not know a good song from a hole in the ground, in your opinion, but he is not blind. This is not exactly a new concept in writer-publisher relations. He knows that you have done something you weren't authorised to do, even if you didn't spend any extra money. If the demo doesn't change his mind, now is the time for you and your co-writer to gang up and try to convince him. Since your publisher is probably in his own office and your co-writer's publisher is in another building, you should have a two-to-one advantage.

This is not always a strictly behind-the-back move. In my days as a staff writer, I routinely threw in an extra song or two on demo sessions. They were often long-shots – a novelty song, a rock song or some other kind of song that didn't fit into the usual pitch patterns. Nevertheless, they needed to be demoed, I felt, so that we would have them when unforeseen pitch opportunities arose. (And they do arise.) Since I had one of the lowest per-song demo costs in the company, my publisher viewed it as making good use of demo time. In his assessment of songs, he left some latitude for the writer being right and himself being wrong. Letting the writer demo a song the writer believed in was one way to hedge his bets.

Again, let me emphasise that this is one particular writer and one particular publisher, who know each other pretty well. Your relationship with your publisher – even if it's the same guy – will be different from mine or any other writer's. In your situation, the publisher may feel that no matter how great the song is that you slipped in on the session, it does not override the fact that you spent his money on something you weren't supposed to, and consequently, from now on you won't be trusted with the responsibility – and more importantly the freedom – to produce your own demos. That's a lot to risk, so be sure your song is great and your publishing situation is good before you do any unscheduled demos.

One is Staff, One is Not

Let's say you're the co-writer who is not signed to a publishing company. If the song is any good, your co-writer's publisher is going to want to control all of the publishing, meaning he's going to ask you for yours. If that's all right with you, if you have confidence in his reaction to the song and his ability to get the song cut, sign it over – but not without making him pay for it with an advance. He's paying your co-writer for songs with a regular retainer, so you ought to be paid, too.

How much advance do you deserve? As much as you can get. The figure will depend on how good the publisher thinks the song is, of course. You can use the co-writer's retainer for comparison and say, "You pay this guy £750 a month and in that time he brings you one song that is this good. I want £750." Good luck on getting that much. But don't be afraid to start high and come down.

Also demand any special treatment – such as reversion options if the song is not cut within a specific time – and refuse any special penalties – such as demo costs being charged back to you – that your co-writer has in his exclusive contract. How strong your bargaining position can be depends on how prepared you are to be your own publisher. If you just stepped off the bus last week and the reason you want to be your own publisher is that you read about it in a book, then your greenness is going to show. In defence of your co-writer's publisher, he does have considerable expenses – writer advances, demo costs and all the expense of renting and staffing an office – and if he's going to be your publishing partner, he wants you to share not just the expense but the effort it takes to get a song cut. Take the advice of a lawyer-turned-songwriter friend of mine: bluff, then settle.

The important thing to remember is that you don't want to make an enemy. You want to make your best deal and then have that publisher working for you and with you to get your song cut. Unless you and your partner are writing one smash hit after another, a testy relationship with his publisher will eventually hurt your songwriting relationship. A couple of so-so songs, and the publisher will tell his writer, "If it's all the same to you, I wish you'd find somebody else to write with. This guy [meaning *you*] is impossible to deal with."

Now switch your point of view for a moment so that *you* are the writer on staff. Your co-writer, in your publisher's opinion, is being a jerk. Through no fault of your own, you're now in a bind. You have to respect your co-writer's right to control his own work, but if it's hurting your success together – if your publisher is cool on your work because he has only half-publishing on it – you may have to take a stand and side with either the publisher or your co-writer, whichever is in your best interest.

Now, switch back to being the unaffiliated writer. If you do publish your own half of the song, you've got to act like a publisher. First of all, you have to sign a co-publishing agreement. In doing that, you have to decide what you're going to do about administration, which involves licensing and collecting, among other things. You may want to sign administration over to your co-publisher (for which he will take a small percentage of your publishing royalty). Under most co-publishing agreements, whichever company pays for the demo (or anything else) will bill the other, so you'll be expected to cover half of all expenses.

Those are some of your legal obligations as a co-publisher. You also have ethical responsibilities – your co-publisher will expect you to provide your share of the resources and the effort necessary to get a song cut. So for the same reason you learned something about writing before you offered yourself as a co-writer, you shouldn't insist on being a co-publisher unless you are prepared to do so. Although you are legally entitled to keep your publishing, a bad co-publishing relationship can damage your chances of getting your song cut, not to mention your co-writing relationship. Take all the factors into consideration, and make the decision that will benefit you most in the long run.

Both Are
Self-Publishers
There are several possibilities here:
1. You both are active publishers. You have already got some songs cut out of

your publishing companies – in which case you are probably already experienced in dealing with the publishing issues that follow in the discussion. If you've never co-published a co-written song before, all you have to do is sign an agreement with your co-publisher and get on with your work.

2. One of you is a novice writer or a part-time writer or a writer who lives in the middle of nowhere, and the other is a full-time songwriter. The full-time writer asks his partner for a larger share of the publishing, as compensation for being the one who is going to end up doing most of the after-writing work. In this case, if you're on the short end, the one who is asked to give up part of his publishing, use your own best judgment to determine if it is a fair deal for both sides. If your co-writer gets a lot of songs cut through his own efforts, then he's a legitimate publisher and deserves some compensation. If you're on the other end, the publishing end, make sure you consider your partner's contributions as well as his legal right to an equal share of the publishing, and don't sacrifice your co-writing relationship to greed.

3. If you're like the majority of struggling songwriters, you and your partner may technically be self-publishers, but not out of choice. You're both looking for a publisher. In this case, the first thing to do is put on your business hat. Aside from the production of the demo (if it comes to that), it's business from here on in. If you have to set up an appointment with your partner – complete with an agenda – in order to make yourselves discuss business, then do it. Re-evaluate your song, asking yourselves *not* just which artist it would be good for, but also which publisher might be the best one for it. Publishing companies have different styles – different types of songs and writers – depending on the different musical tastes of the people who pitch the songs and sign the writers. You'd be wasting your time showing a rock-and-roll song to a straight-arrow gospel publisher. On a more subtle level, it wouldn't make much sense to take a honky tonk singalong to a publishing company that does all of its demos on a drum machine and synthesisr.

Make as informed a choice as you can on which publishers to approach, but more importantly, be in agreement with your partner. It's not necessary for you to shop your song together. One of you may be a better salesman than the other. But you should be able to speak for each other in negotiation. In other words, don't go into a publisher's office trying to interest him in half a song (unless, of course, the other half of the publishing is unavailable). As in any negotiation, you need a plan. You need to know what you're looking for and what you'll settle for. Decide that with your co-writer in advance.

If you are unable to find a publisher, you may want to demo the song – not necessarily a full demo, but something to better present it, something you could play for an artist if the occasion arose. You're now sitting on the fence between being a publisher and being a songwriter – you're still looking for a publisher, but you may end up being the publisher yourself. When you start spending money, you *are* the publisher, so you have to start acting like one. At that point, any lawyer would advise you to get your paperwork in order and sign an agreement with your co-writer/co-publisher. (You can get one from a lawyer or from a friendly publisher.) In reality, most self-publishers view this situation in much the same way as they do the need for a co-writing agreement – they trust each other and usually don't bother to put anything in writing until the song gets cut. As with the co-writing agreement, if you have any doubts about the trustworthiness of your partner, do not hesitate to make him sign.

After you demo the song, you still may want a publisher to pitch it. Assuming your demo is good enough for a publisher to use, you and your co-writer will want to make sure when you sign the song over that you are reimbursed for your demo costs.

If you don't find a publisher, and you do get your song cut, get your paperwork in order as fast as possible. In addition to the agreement you sign with your partner, you will now have such things as performing and mechanical rights registration forms, record licences, foreign administration, sheet music administration, and various other items to deal with. This is the point where you may decide you don't want to be a publisher after all – rather, you want the publishing money but you don't want the administrative headache. Several options are open to you, from strictly administration deals to split publishing deals in which you get not only administration service but possibly some effort to further exploit your song.

All that is basic publishing. Where collaboration is involved, you should, as always, make sure that the percentages in any agreement are accurate. And if you and your partner are considering different administrators, keep in mind that an administration agent may have a stronger negotiating position (for foreign rights or film use, for example) when representing an entire song than when representing just one writer's part. So, communicate with and discuss these matters with your collaborator. Even if he does not want to go along with you, you should keep each other informed.

CHAPTER FIFTEEN

DEMOS AND PITCHING

Whether you publish your part of the song yourself or assign it to a publisher, you and your co-writer now have to think about a demo version to play for artists. Even if you have signed it over to a publisher, giving him ultimate authority and control, setting up and producing the demo session will probably be at least partly your responsibility.

Costs

First you have to agree on the best way to present the song. Some songs – 'Que Sera Sera' or 'Misty,' for example – work fine with just a guitar/vocal or piano/vocal rendition, as long as the quality of the performance and recording is professional, which means having a decent singer, a decent musician and clearly understood lyrics and chords (no kids crying or dogs barking in the background). Others – like 'Billie Jean' or 'I'm So Excited,' which depend as much on production as on melody and lyrics – need a larger production to convey their full potential to a producer or artist.

The extent of the production depends on the song, and unfortunately, it also depends on your budget. If you're the publisher, you have to foot the bill. If you've signed away the song's publishing rights, you'll have to propose a demo within the publisher's perception of what is cost-effective. So regardless of your publishing situation, you'll have to consider demo costs.

As a co-writer/co-publisher, you will expect to be paid your fair share of the royalties on a song, and you are also expected to pay your fair share of the expenses. Back in Chapter 5, I mentioned publishing and demo plans as one of the things to get straight before you start writing. Here's why. Say you co-write a song that needs a rhythm section, a lead instrument and some backing vocal parts – in other words, a studio demo. Let's say you can do it in a friend's basement studio for £150. That's £75 apiece for you and your co-writer. But your co-writer doesn't have £75 to spare. You have two options: 1) do a demo he *can* afford – a rough demo made at home that will not properly showcase the song and will probably doom it to the shelf; or 2) go ahead with the session and foot the whole bill yourself, hoping you'll get your money back when the song gets cut. You start thinking maybe that guy with the eight-track recorder, the drum machine and the synthesiser wouldn't be such a bad guy to co-write with after all.

Reverse the situation, and say your co-writer has a publisher for his half of the song and the publisher wants to demo it. The singer the publisher wants to use is one that the publisher is also interested in producing for a possible record deal, so the publisher wants to do a session of higher-than-average demo quality. It's going to cost £450 for that song. You, as co-publisher, are going to be billed for £225, which is three times the amount you estimated as your cost for an effective demo. But there are other considerations, the main one being the possible inside track to an artist. The decision is not a simple one.

Co-Producing

In the least complicated scenario, one in which one publisher publishes the entire song and that publisher has no limit on budget, the money issue may be settled, but another problem arises – producing the session. You and your co-writer, and to varying degrees, your publisher have to agree on how you want the demo to sound. You may not control the session – especially if you are new at it – but you are entitled to a great deal of input. The publisher legally controls the song now, and he may put it in the hands of a staff demo producer, but you should not let anyone forget that it is still your song, your baby.

Assuming now that you and your co-writer are co-producing the demo, you don't want to go into the studio expecting to do a soul ballad and hear your co-writer instructing the musicians to give it a reggae feel. Believe me, there will be enough surprises and differences of opinion that sprout up from nowhere once you get in the studio; you don't need to bring any more in with you. Plan the session with your co-writer/co-producer in as much detail as possible. It should go without saying: don't do anything – planning or recording – without telling your co-writer.

Once the session starts, you may have to make changes as you go along. The lyric that sounded good on your rough demo now needs a slight melody change to sing right, or another bar or half-bar needs to be inserted before the chorus. Even if you don't have to re-write as you go, you will still have to make creative decisions as the musicians, singers, engineers and everybody else hanging around offer their own creative suggestions.

Where the good of the song has always been the sole deciding factor, now you have to go for the best combination of *efficiency* and *effectiveness*. Now you have to take time into consideration, because in the studio, time is money. For example, if the musicians don't quite understand the feel that you're after, you have to decide whether it is worth the time (i.e., the money) to show them exactly what you want or whether you would be better off letting them do it the way they feel it. Whatever your decision, you have to make it fast. And you have to make it with your co-writer.

Pitching

The songwriter writes the songs and the publisher gets them cut. And pigs fly. Well, sometimes they do. At MCA Music, according to Dave Loggins, "All we've dealt with and deal with is music. We don't have time to go pitching tunes. We're here writing." That is an ideal writer-publisher situation, and it is a rare one. Until you reach the level of success where your songs practically pitch themselves just because your name is on them, you are going to have to do some of the pitching yourself. If you are co-publisher, it is not just to your advantage, it is part of your publishing responsibility to try to get the song cut. If your co-writer is playing your song for every artist who walks into a studio while you're playing golf in the mornings and pricing new cars in the afternoons, you're not holding up your end of the bargain.

This is not to say that if your co-writer gets in to see a producer at CBS, you are obligated to get in to see someone equally important at RCA. As in the writing of the song, you are expected to give your best effort. Your co-writer may know all the top executives at the major labels, and if you don't, it would be less productive for you to approach them. You, on the other hand, may know some rising young artists or musicians or engineers to pitch to.

As in all other aspects of the relationship, get together with your co-writer and discuss who you want to pitch to and how. Agree on a strategy if one is necessary. You don't want to play a song for an artist only to have him say, "I just passed on that song yesterday when your co-writer played it for me. Why are you wasting my time?"

Holds

You also want to stay in communication with your co-writer in case an artist puts a song on hold. Granting a hold and honouring it is not always a simple decision to make. Since a hold is actually the publisher's prerogative – not the writer's – let's assume for the time being that you and your co-writer are also the publishers. If Quincy Jones calls you and asks for a hold on a song for Michael Jackson's next album, no problem. If a year goes by with no album, but the producer has kept in touch, assuring you that you will get the cut, still no problem. The writers and publisher of 'Forty Hour Week' kept it on hold a full year on the promise that Alabama would cut it. Artists of the calibre of Michael Jackson and Alabama are well worth the wait.

But what if a minor artist or an unknown asks for a hold? What if you don't want to grant it, but that unknown is a personal friend of your co-writer's and your refusal puts him in an uncomfortable situation? Do whatever you think is best. If you do decide to continue pitching the song, tell your co-writer that's what you're going to do. You're putting your relationship at enough risk without him finding out about it from a third party.

Publishers will sometimes grant holds and then not honour them, for the simple reason that holds do not always become cuts. If you get caught – if a company goes to the considerable expense of recording, pressing and marketing your song only to find that another artist has beaten them on the market with it – you are going to make somebody quite angry and possibly jeopardise your professional future. There is one way around this, unethical as it may be, and that is to plead ignorance. Blame it on your co-writer. Incorporate such possibilities into your pitch planning so that if conflicts arise, you may truly be innocent. By the time you told your co-writer about a hold, he had already pitched the song to someone else.

Again, this is assuming you are the publisher. Do *not* undermine a hold your publisher has granted – unless, of course, you and your publisher have also planned this strategy of calculated ignorance.

In general, do not undermine a hold. There is too much at risk – your reputation – to employ deceit as standard operating procedure. Honesty, along with good communication between publishers and producers, would be a more productive policy.

If you are like most songwriters, one of the factors that contributed to your decision to be a songwriter was the belief that you could write something at least as good as the junk you hear on the radio. As you get more and more into the business, that self-confidence will turn into frustration as you see inferior songs continue to get cut instead of yours. If your rage doesn't blind you at this point, you will see that writing a good song gets you only halfway to a cut. Many factors other than a song's quality influence the decision to cut it or not. To be competitive, you have to maintain the same perfectionist attitude at the demo and pitch stage that you had during the writing. You can't afford to settle for anything less than the best you can possibly do. In co-writing a song, the sum of the parts is unpredictable – the result of putting two writers together could be more than double the quality of each individual or it could be less than the quality of one writer working alone. But *after* the song is finished, the question marks begin to disappear. As long as you are working together, the efforts of two writers will generally be twice as effective as the efforts of one. Your collaborator shares your desire to get your song cut, so take full advantage of his ambition.

CHAPTER SIXTEEN

MONEY MATTERS

A song earns money from performance royalties (live performance, radio and TV airplay), mechanical royalties (commercial recordings, broadcasts of recorded music), and other licensed uses such as films or commercials. Under your writer/publisher agreement, the songwriter and publisher split all the money that the publisher receives (except in the case of sheet music actually published by your publisher) according to the percentages specified in the contract. If your share of the publishing is 70 percent, then your publisher gets 30 percent. That share is stated on every licence he signs, and the licensees divide up the total payment accordingly. So if you have a 50/50 deal with your collaborator, you'll each end up with 35 percent of your publisher's receipts.

Determining and collecting the fees that provide the funds from which such royalty payments are made is an enormously complex and time-consuming task – one which individual copyright owners could not possibly undertake for themselves. So to make life simpler, a number of organisations collect and distribute royalties on behalf of their publisher and songwriter members. Generally speaking, the most important of these organisations to the songwriter are PRS (the Performing Right Society) and MCPS (the Mechanical Copyright Protection Society).

Performance

The performing right comprises three separate rights: the right to perform a work in public; the right to broadcast that work; and the right to include the work in a cable programme. These rights – which of course apply only to copyright works (you don't need permission to perform Bach's *Matthew Passion* in public) – are the property of the writers involved, until such time, at least, as they are assigned to a publisher, when they become the property of the publisher.

Anyone who wants to perform, broadcast or cable a copyright work has to pay a fee to the copyright owner. This is where the PRS comes in. Its officials negotiate appropriate licence fees with every conceivable kind of user of copyright music – from the BBC and the IBA, who broadcast thousands of hours of music every year, down to small retailers who use background music to create the right sort of 'ambience' in their shops. These fees are then collected, and distributed to writers and publishers on a 'points' basis relating to the frequency of performance or broadcast, the length or nature of each work, and other factors. In other words, Paul McCartney's PRS returns are going to be considerably larger than those of a writer with only 10 hours of airplay to his credit.

You needn't worry too much about the precise way royalties are calculated. What you do need to worry about is getting all of your songs registered with PRS in the first place; if they aren't registered, you won't receive any royalties. If you've got a publishing deal, your publisher should register your songs for you (it's his income too), but it's still worth registering them yourself to make double-sure. If you don't have a publishing deal, there's obviously no alternative to registering your songs yourself. For this you'll need PRS/MCPS Joint Notification Forms (one form for each song), which you can obtain directly from the PRS. It also helps to notify PRS of any airplay or performances of your material that you know about. For instance, if you know that a song of yours got 20 plays on Radio 1 during April, or if you know that George Michael covered one of your songs at his last Wembley concert, send the details to PRS; if they're not aware of those plays or that performance, your performance royalties could be lower than they should be.

Also be aware that the writer/publisher split is crucial. If, as an unknown writer, you agreed to a 50/50 split with your publisher, you won't initially have noticed too much hardship: the performance royalties earned by your songs were minimal anyway , so it will have made little difference to your total income what percentage your publisher was getting – and at the time, you were probably pleased to have any deal at all. But now, 18 months later, you're regularly making the charts, and you're several thousands pounds a year down because you didn't take the trouble to negotiate a fairer publishing deal – say, 60/40 in your favour. As an unknown writer you won't get as good a deal as Paul McCartney, but you owe it to yourself and your partner to stick out for the best you can get.

Mechanicals   Mechanical royalties – known as 'mechanicals' – are paid to copyright owners in return for the right to record their work. For instance, if one of your songs is commercially recorded, the record company must pay you – or you and your publisher, if you have one – a royalty for the privilege. The current statutory royalty rate is 6¼ percent of the retail price (excluding VAT) of the record. So if you have one cut on an album of 10 tracks, you will get one tenth of 6¼ percent of the retail price of every album sold – or, in the case of the smaller record companies, of every album *pressed*.

Mechanicals can be paid directly to the publisher or songwriter by the record company, but you'll probably find it more convenient to join MCPS and let them do the work of collection for you. In addition to collecting from record companies, MCPS negotiates 'blanket agreements' with all UK broadcasters, allowing them to record MCPS members' works into TV and radio progrmmes in exchange for an annual blanket royalty fee. They also negotiate licences with film and video companies, advertising agencies, background music operators, record importers and anyone else who records MCPS members' works.

If you publish your own songs, you *could* do all of this yourself, but have you really got the time? If you have a publisher, he may do his own negotiation and collection, or he may let MCPS do it for him. If he does use MCPS, double-check that any recordings of your songs are registered with them. And once again, if you do assign your copyright to a publisher, make sure that you negotiate the best royalty split you can.

Publishing Situations

Even when co-writers get paid fairly and equally for a song, in some situations, one writer appears to reap more from his work than the other. Say you write for a small publishing company that operates from hit to distant hit on a shoestring budget. Your co-writer is on the staff of one of the larger, more successful publishers in town. You're both getting a retainer of £800 a month against mechanicals. The song you co-wrote becomes a hit single from a big-selling album, and your co-writer's publisher, knowing from the charts and from record sales reports that a certain amount of money will be coming in within the next year, willingly renegotiates his retainer up to £1,200 a month. Your publisher also knows that that money is coming in, but he simply can't afford to raise your retainer. You (and your publisher, too) must hang on for six months or more until that money is actually received. Since your retainer is less than your co-writer's, you will be 'out of the hole' and into mechanical royalties on the song before he will, but that's not much consolation now. You could really use the extra £400 a month. In this case, life, rather than payment, is unfair.

An even greater perceived inequity is the case in which you sign away your publishing for a small advance and your collaborator holds on to his. He now gets considerably more money than you do. If the cut is *not* a single (no airplay money) and your retainer has you in the hole to your publisher for, say, ten thousand pounds, then you're not going to see any money at all until the ten thousand is paid back. You conveniently forget that your co-writer did not have the advantage and security of a retainer all this time and that he had to shoulder all the responsibilities and expenses that go along with being his own publisher. All you see now is that he's making money and you're not. This is especially frustrating if your publisher never liked the song in the first place, never pitched it, and is now (in your opinion, at least) getting a free ride at your expense. All you can do is remember that what you perceive as your bad fortune was your own choice. The writers' payments are equal. Complain if you can find someone to listen, but (need I say it again?) don't let it affect your writing.

Principle vs. Money

You and your collaborator write a song and it becomes a hit. You make a nice sum of money. You buy a new house and a new car. Now an advertising agency has called you (actually, your publisher) wanting to adapt your song and use it as a jingle to pitch a product. You don't have to be a star and appear in the ads, like Lionel Richie or Michael Jackson, for the offer to be substantial. Your publisher asks you what you want to do about the offer. (Legally, the publisher doesn't need the permission of the writers, but in any case involving a publisher with a conscience, the writers would be given the option of turning it down.) Your song is going to be known from now on as a beer commercial, but for a hundred and fifty thousand pounds, who cares? It's already run its course on the charts. Anything else is gravy. You'd probably say "Yes." I would.

But what if your partner is a devout Moslem or a recovering alcoholic? He's already made a great deal of money off the song in its original form, and he is vehemently opposed to promoting the consumption of alcohol. You argue that if he feels so guilty about it, he can donate his entire share – plus, you'll even tithe yours – to his mosque or to Alcoholics Anonymous. He steadfastly refuses. It's going to be hard for you in the future to sit down face-to-face and try to write another hit song with a guy who has cost you a hundred and fifty thousand pounds.

The hypothetical part of that situation pits a personal principle versus an unsuitable product. In another example, artistic principles come into play. John Cougar Mellencamp and George Green wrote 'Hurts So Good,' which was a huge pop hit for Mellencamp. An American ketchup company wanted to use the song in a commercial for some sort of sauce. Here again, it's legally the publisher's decision, but he put it to Mellencamp. Mellencamp is a huge rock-and-roll star. He makes tons of money as a performer, a recording artist, and the writer of most of the songs on his albums. Green is not doing badly by himself, co-writing with Mellencamp and getting other cuts as well, but he's not in the same income bracket. Since Mellencamp happens to have a larger writer's percentage than Green on 'Hurts So Good,' the publisher put the commercial offer to Mellencamp first. He passed, presumably because he didn't need the money and he felt a commercial would compromise his artistic integrity.

From this point on, rumour makes for a better example than fact. I would be incensed with Mellencamp, and according to rumours, Green was incensed but powerless. But in reality, Green says, the issue was never put before him, and he didn't care one way or the other. "I'm not real big on using songs in commercials," he explained. Then he added, "I could use a half-a-million dollars as much as anybody else, but I'd rather make my money other ways."

The potential income from advertising or other licensed uses, such as film soundtracks, is more than just icing on the earnings cake. It's possible that the icing could actually outweigh the cake. The money is great enough to make a significant difference to most songwriters' financial security. Yet the possibility of a commercial is so remote that you wouldn't normally sound out a collaborator on it before you started writing together. If, however, your collaborator does veto such an opportunity, the next time you start a song, you'll want to get in a little dig, maybe say, "Now before we get going, what if somebody wants this one for a deodorant commercial? Are there any other products you wouldn't take a million quid to endorse?" Or you may not want to write with him at all. You may want to see what his heirs' views are on the subject, and if they are favourable, you may want to have him declared incompetent to handle his own affairs.

Promotion Extortion

You and your co-writer have a cut that is under consideration for a single. Word comes from the artist's manager that the publisher of another cut has offered to spend £2,000 on independent promotion if his song is selected as the single instead of yours. (That means the rival publisher will hire someone to call major radio stations or in some other way to complement and amplify the efforts of the record company's promotion staff.) The artist's manager claims he is telling you this as your friend, and that the final decision is not his but the record company's. If the message is not clearly stated, it is clearly implicit: match the offer or forget the single.

A variation on this gambit is for the call to come when the record has been on the charts for a few weeks and is supposedly going to lose its momentum unless extra promotion help is called in – at the publisher's expense, of course. Whether or not you should accede is debatable. Some publishers kick in the money. Others feel that if the record is dying in the minds of the label's promotion staff, then no amount of independent promotion can revive it, and the money could be better spent by dangling it in front of the record company staff as a bonus incentive – "Get it into the Top 10 and there's an extra £500 in it for everybody."

But that is not the issue here. If you and your collaborator co-publish the song, and one of you does not have the money, you have a conflict that could damage your writing relationship. Even if you both have publishers and the decision is thus out of your hands, you may not be unaffected. If your publisher wants to kick in and your co-writer's publisher thinks it's either unaffordable or unwise, you will eventually have a problem in your writing relationship. If it happens again with the next song the two of you write, your publisher may ask you to look for a co-writer whose publisher isn't afraid to shell out a little money to get a hit.

As with commercial possibilities, the issue of hiring independent promotion for a single is a long way in the distance when you first sit down to write with someone. In fact, that is probably *not* the time to discuss it, since opinions and plans may change according to changes in the financial position of the writer or publisher involved. Nevertheless, it doesn't hurt to know your partner's general feelings on these issues.

CHAPTER SEVENTEEN

SHARING SUCCESS
AND REJECTION

In business and in sports, the 'team player' is often considered to be more valuable than the talented individual for whom personal glory is the primary goal and the fortunes of the team are incidental. Even sportsmen who compete as individuals routinely credit success to a team effort. When you collaborate with another writer, you form a team – even if it's just for one song. You share your talents with each other in order to write a good song, and the sharing should continue after the song is written.

Recognising Credit

In an interview, Marvin Hamlisch talked at length about 'The Way We Were,' *A Chorus Line,* and his many other successful works. He talked about the joys of collaboration in writing for a show – collaboration with costumes, lights, scenery and dialogue. He was even so humble as to say that the programme for *A Chorus Line* should have credited first the director and choreographer, and then said 'Music by Marvin Hamlisch, with many suggestions.' Funny, I remember Barbra Streisand singing words to 'The Way We Were' and I remember the actors singing – not humming – the songs in *A Chorus Line,* but nowhere in this five-page spread does he even mention a lyric or lyricist. On behalf of Alan Bergman and Marilyn Keith Bergman ('The Way We Were') and Edward Klevan (*A Chorus Line*) and all the collaborators of the world, I'd like to say "Thanks, Marv."

Hamlisch's attitude goes farther back than Hamlisch himself does, to the beginnings of collaboration, or at least to the point where the terms *lyricist* and *composer* were first applied to songwriters. The terms themselves are of unequal standing; they do not simply mean 'a person who writes words' and 'a person who writes music.' *Lyric* connotes something music-related, and if only in terms of rhythm and sonority, music-dependent. The work of the composer, on the other hand, can exist with or without lyrics. Mozart is called a composer. So is Jerome Kern. If Dylan Thomas is a poet, why is Oscar Hammerstein II not? Why isn't a lyricist's counterpart called a melodist (aside from the fact that *melodist* already has a different, although archaic, meaning)?

This seems a rather petty, academic point, but I believe it is indicative of a superior attitude shared by many composers, based on an erroneous conclusion they have drawn from the fact that the majority of lyricists prefer to craft the words around the music. It's generally accepted that Vincent Youmans had no respect for lyricists. It's been written that Jerome Kern would not 'give an extra note,' would not add to or otherwise change a single note of his melody to accommodate a lyric. Yes, these are great composers, but *no*, they were not any greater than the lyricists they worked with.

More recently, Burt Bacharach was asked in interview, "Which is more important, lyrics or melody?" He replied, "Nobody whistles a lyric." This is the same Burt Bacharach who was featured in a TV special in the sixties on which, as I recall, he did not *whistle* anything – melodies or lyrics. He and his guests *sang* lyrics to all his melodies, although (again, as I recall) the man who wrote all those lyrics, Hal David, was not once acknowledged.

If, despite his own evidence to the contrary, Bacharach would still insist on placing the composer above the lyricist, I would refer him to Oscar Hammerstein's wife. A famous Broadway anecdote tells of Mrs. Hammerstein's hearing someone at a party say that Jerome Kern wrote 'Ol' Man River.' She explained that all Kern wrote was "Da dum dum deedum"; Hammerstein wrote "[Dat] Ol' Man River."

One notable exception is Jule Styne, a composer who believes the 'pay dirt' is in the lyrics. As he explained in his autobiography, you may walk away from a show humming a tune, but you would never have listened to it long enough to remember it if the lyric had not caught and held your attention.

Whether it's lyric versus melody or one writer's saying his chorus is much more important to the song than his co-writer's verses, a superior attitude from either partner can do nothing but harm a relationship. If there is any collaboration at all, the song should be considered a joint work (even if it isn't legally), a work created by all the collaborators *together,* with individual contributions now inseparable. That is a legal viewpoint, granted, but it would be good to incorporate it into your sense of professional courtesy.

Taking Credit   One of the nice aspects of collaboration is that you can take credit for things you didn't actually do. Even if you happened to have a bad day and didn't contribute much to a certain song, when the time comes to be interviewed or to accept an award, you can proudly state, "I'm the co-writer of that song . . . " You can act as though your contribution were equal to everyone else's. Just don't get too specific about your great contributions. Smile and say "we" when you talk about the writing of the song, expound on such subjects as the true collaborative process and the theory of songwriting, and take the compliments graciously.

Sharing Rejection   Remember that you have created a joint work. Just because your co-writer wrote the entire melody does not mean it is his fault entirely if the song is rejected by a producer on the grounds that the melody is not strong enough. You were there – maybe not when the melody was written, but when it was agreed that it would be the final melody. It may well be that the song does need a stronger melody, but that is something you say *diplomatically* and *privately* to your partner. Publicly, you say, "I guess *we* just didn't quite hook it."

At the very start of this book, on the list of advantages of collaboration was the idea that rejection is easier to take when it is shared. If your song is rejected time and again for no particular reason, you may begin to doubt its worth. Your publisher has already put it on the shelf. If your co-writer still believes in the song, his support and reassurance could renew your faith. If, on the other hand, he has also begun to doubt the song's worth, it's time to re-evaluate – together. You don't have to decide that it's a bad song; you do have to admit that it's not going to be cut the way it is. If it can't be fixed through a rewrite or a new demo, chalk it up to experience.

Take a positive attitude toward rejection. With your partner, analyse and learn from the experience. Even if a song has to be shelved, go at the next one with a stronger determination.

Sticking Together

The theory that drew you to collaborate in the first place – two writers are stronger than one – applies not just to your writing, but to your publishing and other business dealings as well. Through successes and, especially, through failures, it is important to stick together, to channel your energies in the same direction. Your successes will be sweeter and your rejections less bitter.

CHAPTER EIGHTEEN

GROWING TOGETHER
OR APART

Collaboration has been likened to marriage, and with good reason. Success in marriage is dependent on a compatible combination of personalities and physical qualities; success in collaboration requires a compatible combination of talent and personality – two complex qualities that are difficult to measure and analyse. The complexity of collaboration is compounded over time because those elements are ever-changing. The changes, even when they have a positive effect on the relationship, may nevertheless cause problems. As Pam Rose explained, "You go through everything you go through in a [romantic] relationship. You go through growth, and you know, sometimes change in growth is painfully difficult for one person, much less two people and three people."

Here are some of the ways your collaborative relationship may grow and change.

Together
If everything goes right, you and your partner grow stronger working together. Your songs get better and your success gets bigger. Burt Bacharach explained it: "As you continue to write with someone, you get the working formula down. The songs get better as you know the other's moves better. That gives you confidence."

But no two individuals have the same growth rate. You and your partner have had a respectable amount of success writing commercial soul ballads, but lately you've found yourself listening exclusively to jazz albums or musicals. You feel you have more to say now, musically and lyrically, than you can fit into a three-minute radio slot. You've experienced success; now you want a higher level of artistic recognition. You want to do a longer, more serious piece of work – a show or a concept album, something that will last longer than a 20-week run on the charts. Your partner is no musical illiterate, but he's perfectly satisfied doing what you've been doing. It's going to take him a few more years to get bored and catch up to your new ambitions – if he ever does. For the time being, the two of you are probably going to argue more than you're going to write.

That's an obvious example, but growth as a songwriter can be more subtle than wanting to branch out into a new style. It could be just a desire to write better. Pat Bunch talked about the problems within a relationship when one person grows. She said she and Pam Rose and Mary Ann Kennedy were working along as usual when, "All of a sudden, it was like Mary Ann wasn't turned on. I could tell she wasn't. She was tired of what we were doing. And it took me a while to figure that out. I couldn't grasp that. I couldn't figure out why she wasn't responding to these things we were working on. They *were* all fine. Why weren't they now? We didn't really write much for two or three months. Then I finally figured it out. I showed her something that was such a jump in the writing that her response told me. She was no longer interested in *this* kind of a spectrum. It was *here* [at a different level] now and it was better."

Apart

While the most common tendency among songwriters who collaborate is to grow more dependent on co-writers, some writers will grow in the opposite direction. Frank Loesser was one of Hollywood's most successful lyricists until 1941, when he showed some friends his lyrics to 'Praise the Lord and Pass the Ammunition.' He usually worked with a dummy melody, and that was what he played. His friends assured him that the melody was no dummy, and from then on Loesser wrote both lyrics and music. Carole King described herself as an abysmal lyricist when she met her husband/lyricist Gerry Goffin, but after their marriage and their writing team broke up, she achieved even greater success writing alone. Stephen Sondheim's lyric credits include the all-time favourite *West Side Story*, but his reputation as the man who stretched the boundaries of musical theatre was made later, writing alone.

John Lennon and Paul McCartney had as unique a career as collaborators as they did performers. Their common goal was the success of their band rather than success just as a songwriting team. Instead of becoming more and more enmeshed and dependent on each other and growing together as a team, they grew as individual writers, each gaining more self-confidence in his ability to write a song alone. They went from face-to-face collaboration, to helping each other finish a song, to writing completely alone. In the final stage, their only collaboration was on a song's credit line.

None of the usual reasons for the break-up of the team apply to Lennon and McCartney. One of them did *not* burn out or slack off. Nor was there any significant difference in lifestyles that affected their collaboration. Their writing together did *not* become stale; it became unnecessary. I may be reading too much into Lennon's comments in his *Playboy* interview, but I suspect that the original agreement between Lennon and McCartney to share credit on all their songs was at Lennon's invitation, based on McCartney's superior musicianship and on the fact (at least the inference by Lennon) that McCartney was already writing songs. In other words, McCartney was ahead of Lennon and a 50/50 partnership would benefit Lennon. Later (this is still my speculation), Lennon no longer felt he needed McCartney, and he was the one who announced he would no longer credit McCartney on his songs.

For whatever reason, the Lennon-McCartney equal credit agreement had a surprising benefit once their need for each other lessened. It allowed them to be competitive and to develop the particular areas in which each thought he was lacking. But because of the equal compensation, there were none of the resentful feelings – at least not for financial reasons – that can arise in such competition.

In the end, their individual competitiveness did prove to be a more powerful force than their collaboration. Their last album, *Abbey Road*, is divided into Paul's side and John's side. The shared writing credits ended when The Beatles ended, but the collaboration had been dead for years.

With Others The similarity between collaboration and marriage stops when it comes to multiple partners. Although some teams do remain exclusive, many songwriters prefer to work with more than one regular partner. "It's hard to write with the same person and keep the creative spark going, as it is hard to live with the same person and keep the creative spark going," according to Cynthia Weil. Consequently, she and Barry Mann have each worked with, and have had considerable success with, other collaborators. They find that that sort of 'outside contact' has a positive effect on their work together. "When we write together again," Weil said, "there's a whole new energy – a fresh approach."

For mature, self-confident songwriters, such unproductive emotions as jealousy and possessiveness should *not* be a factor when partners are changing. Will Jennings says a year or two might go between writing sessions with his regular partners (Richard Kerr, Joe Sample and Steve Winwood). About getting together again, he said, "We just pick up where we left off."

Ending When it comes to ending a collaboration, the emotions involved make it once again similar to a marriage. It's easy to make a general statement about when it's time to quit: when the relationship isn't working, it's time to quit. But because each relationship is different, just as in marriage, it's difficult to say what circumstances qualify as 'not working.'

To John Bettis, it means that the success is not there, even though the songs may be: "The single hardest thing is stopping a relationship that you love because it's not succeeding. When you have a relationship that you believe in, that answers all your emotional needs, where you believe in the songs, you're demoing the hell out of them, you write together for two or three years and you don't get a single record, that is a tragedy of the worst sort." Barry Mann concurs: "Sometimes you can love what you're doing with someone and you can love them, but if there isn't any success, you have to move on," he said. "Especially now, you really have to go for the throat if you want to sell."

The more obvious reason for ending a relationship is that the songs are *not* there – the work has become stale. *Stale* is the exact word Neil Sedaka used to describe his work with his long-time collaborator Howie Greenfield. They had decided to quit writing together, but they made the most out of that decision. "He came to my apartment and told me he had a present for me," Sedaka recalled. "I looked around and didn't see any present, and Howie explained that his present was a title – 'Our Last Song Together.' " Sedaka happened to have a melody and they wrote the song, incorporating all their earlier titles into the lyric. Then they cried. Then, because Greenfield had one more day before he was leaving town, they got together for one more last song and wrote 'Love Will Keep Us Together,' which later became a hit for the Captain and Tennille.

If you and your partner both agree that the work is stale, then you may be able to fix the problem without a permanent split. Mann and Weil recharge their creativity by working separately with other writers. Dennis Morgan and Rhonda 'Kye' Fleming, in the later stages of their relationship, began working *together* with other writers, getting that "little extra something," as Morgan calls it, from a third writer.

In other cases, the work may still be good – when the work gets done. But changes in the individual writers have made it difficult or impossible for the relationship to function. Burt Bacharach and Hal David split because their lifestyles began to diverge: Bacharach was spending more and more time in Hollywood (and eventually moved there), while David remained in New York. Their split was later widened to the point that they were not on speaking terms, as a result of their difference of opinion in settling a lawsuit Dionne Warwick filed against them.

A similar case, but with the opposite ending, is that of Roger Greenaway and Roger Cook. Their split was caused by factors totally beyond their control. They were quite happy working together, but their success was so great that, according to Greenaway, they were penalised for it. He recounts an incident to illustrate: "We had a situation at one time where we had Number One, Two, and Four on the charts, and we had another record out. I had the producer of *Top of the Pops* asking me if he could have this particular act on the show next week. And when I told him it was us, he said, 'Well, I'm sorry, I can't use it because we're getting accused of giving you too much airtime.' Roger [Cook] didn't like that, and he was right, of course."

Consequently, Cook eventually decided to leave England and move to Nashville. Greenaway did not want to leave England. "Our partnership never really ended, because we didn't fall out with each other," Greenaway says. But unlike Will Jennings and his partners, when Greenaway and Cook get together now, they don't pick up where they left off. "Now we tend to rap rather than write, forget that we're here to write," Greenaway says.

For some great writing teams, health is the factor in the break-up. After Frederick Loewe's heart attack in 1958, he became more lackadaisical in tending to his writing responsibilities. His last work with Alan Lerner was *Camelot*, which they finished in 1960. Richard Rodgers lost both of his partners to poor health – Lorenz Hart, who recognised his own decline, and the successor he recommended to Rodgers, Oscar Hammerstein.

Moving On

As you can see, especially in these last two examples, the ending of a relationship can be devastating, emotionally as well as professionally. "I am permanently grieved," was Rodgers's entire statement upon Hammerstein's death in 1960. Lerner said, after Loewe's heart attack, "There will never be another Fritz. Writing will never again be as much fun. A collaboration as intense as ours inescapably had to be complex. But I loved him more than I understood or misunderstood him, and I know he loved me more than he understood or misunderstood me."

Even without the incapacitation of a partner, the emotional blow of a break-up can be severe. When Morgan and Fleming finally did split up, they had written by Morgan's estimate six hundred songs, and they were financially secure. According to Morgan, Fleming was burning out. She formed her own publishing company and she quit writing for a time. Morgan had begun to feel restless, to feel a need for growth that eventually resulted in regular trips to London to collaborate with British writers. And like Fleming, he had a long-term plan to be a publisher (which he has since implemented successfully). The break-up of the team "worked out great," Morgan says now, but at the time, he felt his plans and his career were deeply threatened. "There were strange feelings for a while," he recalls. "Scared me a little bit, put the damn pressure on me, pressure to beat the syndrome of 'Now they've split up, they've had a great career, go to your corner now.' I felt pressure – maybe it was totally inside myself – to show people that I really did mean business, and I'm moving on, and the biggest hits were yet to come."

Morgan acted fast. He took all of 22 hours not only to write a new song with Don Pfrimmer, but to get it cut by Marie Osmond (who was being produced by his publisher). "That broke the Kye-Dennis syndrome," he said, "that neither one of us could have hits without the other."

Breaking up a collaborative relationship can be as traumatic as breaking up a love affair, but the similarities don't stop there. Most people with broken hearts eventually fall in love again, and most songwriters find that the break-up of a partnership is not the end of the world. Bacharach's new partners have included Paul Anka and Carole Bayer Sager. Sedaka said he found "what I needed – a young, poetic, avant-garde lyricist with sensitivity and feeling" named Phil Cody, and their first efforts comprised Sedaka's *Solitaire* album. Morgan quickly took Steve Davis up on an earlier co-writing invitation, with successful results. Fleming, too, after her hiatus, returned to the charts with new collaborators, among them Don Schlitz. Alan Jay Lerner went on to write 'On a Clear Day You Can See Forever' with Burton Lane. Richard Rodgers had more difficulty after the loss of his partner – he wrote his own lyrics for *No Strings* – but he eventually did find new collaborators, among them Stephen Sondheim.

Two options other than finding a new partner are available to the broken-hearted collaborator – write alone or quit writing. If neither of them is attractive to you, then it's time to get over any emotional problems and get on with your career. Start with a positive attitude. Look at your past work *not* as the ultimate end, but as a stepping stone along a path of continuous growth.

AFTERWORD

I had no idea when I started that I was going to have so much to say about collaboration. I thought you just sat down with somebody and wrote a song. And ultimately, that *is* still what you have to do. I hope this book has made it a little easier for you.

I have nothing more to add, but there are a few things worth repeating.

First of all, you have to work to make collaboration work. The advantages are not automatic. Despite the valid opinions of those who don't like to co-write, two writers *can* be better than one – *if* those two are combining their strengths and pulling together rather than working against each other. Every writer has something to offer, so take advantage. That's the basic reason for collaboration.

Secondly – and this applies to co-writing, writing alone, digging ditches and managing corporations – *do not settle for anything less than the best*.

And finally, if you haven't already put this book down and got started on the business of collaboration, get to it now. You can't learn it any other way than by doing it.

Oh, and one other thing: if you have a good idea for a song, give me a call.

APPENDIX

WRITERS AND COLLABORATORS

Writer (collaborator)	Song or Show
Pat Alger (Fred Koller, Bill Dale)	First Time Love Going Gone
Harold Arlen (Ted Koehler) (Johnny Mercer)	Stormy Weather Blues in the Night
Nickolas Ashford & Valerie Simpson	Solid as a Rock Reach Out and Touch (Some- body's Hand) You're All I Need to Get By
Irving Berlin	God Bless America *Yankee Doodle Dandy*
Chuck Berry	Maybellene Memphis
John Bettis (Michael Clarke) (Jonathan Lind)	Slow Hand Crazy For You
Tom Brasfield (Walt Aldridge) (Walt Aldridge)	There's No Getting Over Me Holding Her and Loving You
Felice & Boudleaux Bryant	Bye Bye Love Rocky Top All I Have to Do Is Dream Love Hurts
Sammy Cahn (Jule Styne) (James Van Heusen)	Three Coins in a Fountain High Hopes
George M. Cohan	Over There Harrigan
Roger Cook (Bobby Wood) (John Prine)	Talking in Your Sleep Love is on a Roll
Hal David (Archie Jordan) (Burt Bacharach) (Burt Bacharach)	It Was Almost Like a Song What the World Needs Now Walk on By

Mac Davis	Baby, Baby, Don't Get Hooked on Me I Believe in Music
Bob Dylan	Blowin' in the Wind Just Like a Woman
Steve Earle (Ron Kling)	Guitar Town Nowhere Road
Jerry Foster & Bill Rice	Ain't She Something Else For a Minute There Let's Put it All Back Together Again
Dallas Frazier	Elvira There Goes My Everything
Ira Gershwin (George Gershwin) (Harold Arlen)	Lady, Be Good The Man That Got Away
Randy Goodrum	Bluer Than Blue You Needed Me
George Green (John Mellencamp) (Rick Giles)	Hurts So Good Come on In
Roger Greenaway (Roger Cook)	You've Got Your Troubles, I've Got Mine
(Roger Cook, Allan Clarke)	Long Cool Woman
Tom T. Hall	I Love The Year Clayton Delaney Died
E. Y. 'Yip' Harburg (Harold Arlen) (Jay Gorney)	Somewhere Over the Rainbow Brother, Can You Spare a Dime?
Jimbeau Hinson (Roy August) (Steve Earle)	Broken Trust I'm Settin' Fancy Free Hillbilly Highway
Eddie Holland, Lamont Dozier & Brian Holland	I Can't Help Myself You Keep Me Hanging On I'll Be There
Harlan Howard (Hank Cochran)	Busted I Fall to Pieces
Mick Jagger & Keith Richard	Satisfaction Start Me Up

Will Jennings
  (Steve Winwood)   Higher Love
  (Joe Sample)   Street Life
  (Richard Kerr)   Looks Like We Made It

Al Kasha   The Morning After
& Joel Hirschhorn   We May Never Love Like This
                             Again

Jack Keller (Gerry Goffin)   Run to Him
  (Howard Greenfield)   Everybody's Somebody's Fool
  (Diane Hildebrand)   Easy Come, Easy Go

Richard Kerr
  (Will Jennings)   Somewhere in the Night
  (Scott English)   Mandy (originally Brandy)

Carole King   You've Got a Friend
  (Gerry Goffin)   Up on the Roof
  (Gerry Goffin)   Chains

Fred Knobloch (Dan Tyler)   The Whole World's in Love
                            When You're Lonely
  (Dan Tyler)   Baby's Got a New Baby

Fred Koller   This Dream's on Me
  (Lewis Anderson)   Will It Be Love by Morning

Kris Kristofferson   For the Good Times
                            Why Me Lord
  (Fred Foster)   Me and Bobby McGee

Alan Jay Lerner   *My Fair Lady*
& Frederick Loewe   *Camelot*

Jerry Lieber & Mike Stoller   Love Potion Number 9
                            Hound Dog

Jay Livingston   Mona Lisa
& Ray Evans   Theme to *Bonanza*
                            Theme to *Mr. Ed*
                            Que Sera Sera
                            Silver Bells

Frank Loesser   *Guys and Dolls*
                            Praise the Lord and
                              Pass the Ammunition

Dave Loggins   Please Come to Boston
  (Don Schlitz, Lisa Silver) Forty-Hour Week
  (Lisa Silver)   Maggie's Dream

Barry Manilow (Marty Panzer) Copacabana
  (Adrienne Anderson)   Daybreak

Barry Mann
  (Cynthia Weil) — Here You Come Again
  (Dan Hill) — Sometimes When We Touch

Peter McCann — The Right Time of the Night
  (Mark Wright) — Nobody Falls Like a Fool

Joe Melson (Roy Orbison) — Only the Lonely
  (Roy Orbison) — Crying
  (Roy Orbison) — Running Scared

Johnny Mercer (Henry Mancini) — Moon River
  (Harold Arlen) — That Old Black Magic
  (Harry Warren) — Jeepers, Creepers

Roger Miller — Dang Me
King of the Road
Big River

Dennis Morgan
  (Rhonda 'Kye' Fleming) — Nobody
  (Rhonda 'Kye' Fleming) — I Was Country (When Country Wasn't Cool)
  (Steve Davis) — Just a Little Love
  (Simon Climie) — I Knew You Were Waiting for Me

Bob Morrison
  (Patti Ryan, Wanda Mallette) — Looking for Love
  (Jim Zerface, Bill Zerface) — Angels, Roses and Rain
  (Debbie Hupp) — You Decorated My Life
  (Johnny MacRae) — Shine On

Don Pfrimmer
  (Archie Jordan) — Drifter
  (Dennis Morgan, Mike Reid) — She Keeps the Home Fires Burning

Cole Porter — Begin the Beguine
Anything Goes

Kent Robbins — Love Is Alive
(I'm a) Stand By My Woman Man
  (Dave Gibson) — Heart Trouble

Richard Rodgers
  (Oscar Hammerstein II) — *The Sound of Music*
  (Oscar Hammerstein II) — *South Pacific*
  (Lorenz Hart) — *Pal Joey*
  (Stephen Sondheim) — *Do I Hear a Waltz?*

Fred Rose — Blue Eyes Crying in the Rain
  (Hank Williams) — Kaw-liga

Pam Rose & Mary Ann Kennedy
  (Pat Bunch) Me Against the Night
  (Pat Bunch, Todd Cerney) I'll Still Be Loving You
  (Don Goodman) Ring on Her Finger

Troy Seals
  (Eddie Setser) Seven Spanish Angels
  (Mentor Williams) When We Make Love

Neil Sedaka Lonely Nights
  (Howard Greenfield) Breaking Up Is Hard to Do
  (Phil Cody) Bad Blood

Don Schlitz The Gambler
  (Russell Smith) The Old School
  (Paul Overstreet) On the Other Hand

Thom Schuyler Sixteenth Avenue
  (Paul Overstreet) I Fell in Love Again Last Night

Arthur Schwartz Dancing in the Dark
& Howard Dietz You and the Night and the Music

John Schweers Daydreams About Night Things
No One Mends a Broken Heart

Whitey Shafer (Lefty Frizzell) That's the Way Love Goes
  (Lefty Frizzell) I Never Go Around Mirrors

Paul Simon Bridge Over Troubled Water
The Sound of Silence

Tom Snow (Cynthia Weil) He's So Shy
  (Dean Pitchford) Let's Hear It for the Boy

Stephen Sondheim *Sunday in the Park With George*
  (Leonard Bernstein) *West Side Story*

Bruce Springsteen Born in the U.S.A.
Fire

Jule Styne (Stephen Sondheim) *Gypsy*
  (Sammy Cahn) I'll Walk Alone

James Taylor Fire and Rain
Carolina in My Mind

Allen Toussaint Tell It Like It Is
Southern Nights

Jim Webb By the Time I Get to Phoenix
McArthur Park
The Highwayman

Cynthia Weil (Barry Mann) You've Lost That Lovin' Feelin'
  (Quincy Jones) A Time for Love

GLOSSARY

Advance: 'up front' money paid to a writer or artist that will be deducted from future royalties.

Artist: a recording artist; a singer.

Blanket licence: the type of licence granted by PRS and MCPS to broadcasting organisations, under which the licensee pays one fee for the use of all registered works.

Bridge: the part of a song that departs musically and lyrically from the verse or chorus.

Catalogue: all the songs a publisher contols; or all the songs a songwriter has written.

Changes: chord changes; the chord structure of a song.

Chords: the harmonic elements of a song.

Chord symbols: the configurations that designate chords; for example, *D* is a D Major chord, *C7* is a C Seventh, *Gm* is G Minor, *Fmaj7* is F Major Seventh, *B♭dim* is B-flat Diminished, *G#sus4* is G-sharp Suspended Fourth; a slash between two chords, such as *Dm7/G,* indicates a bass note other than the normal bass note of the first chord, in this case a D Minor Seventh with a G bass note.

Chorus: a repeated section of a song, usually with the same lyric each time.

Copyright: legal protection for and ownership of a song; or a song itself, usually a song that has made a lot of money.

Cover: a recording of a song, usually not the first recording.

Cut: to record; or a recording.

Demo: short for *demonstration recording;* a recorded version of a song, not meant to be released to the general public, designed to show how the song would sound as a record.

Engineer: the person responsible for the technical end of a recording session, for getting the sound on tape.

Hold: a notification of intent to record a song, made by a producer, artist, or A&R person, and an implicit request that the publisher does not pitch the song or license the song to any other artist.

Hook: the part of a song, either lyrical or melodic, that is the most identifiable and memorable, often the title.

Label: record company.

Licence: an agreement in which a publisher allows a specified use of a song, such as performance, mechanical or synchronisation (see individual listings).

Master: the recorded version that will be released to the public.

Mechanical licence: a licence granted by the publisher to record and sell a song on a record, tape, compact disc or some other 'mechanical' configuration. A publisher can refuse to license a recording of a song if it has never been previously released.

Melody: the tune of a song.

Middle eight: the bridge of a song.

Mix: the final stage of a recording session, in which all the instrumental and vocal parts are adjusted and processed into a stereo (two-track) version.

Modulation: changing of keys in the middle of a song.

Multitrack recording: putting each instrument and vocal part on its own separate track so that they can be individually adjusted or replaced later.

Performance licence: a licence for the public performance of a song, granted to radio and TV stations, concert halls, clubs, etc. (see *Blanket licence*).

Performing Right Society: the society that licenses, collects and distributes performance royalties.

Pitch: an attempt to interest an artist or producer in recording a song.

Producer: the person responsible for the making of a record; responsibilities include finding songs, contracting the studio and musicians, and directing the recording session and the mix session.

Publisher: a person (or company) who has been assigned or licensed all or some of the rights to a song by a songwriter, in return for a percentage of the royalties received on the song; it is the publisher's job (though not his contractural obligation) to exploit the song, primarily by getting it recorded (ironically, most publishers sub-contract the actual publishing of a song – the printing and selling of sheet music).

Publishing rights: in a strict sense, the right to make and sell a printed version of a song; also refers to the rights assigned or licensed by the songwriter in a standard publishing contract, which include *all* copyright rights.

Release (verb and noun): to put a record out; or the actual record that is on the market.

Retainer: a regular advance, paid to staff writers.

Riff: a memorable melodic or rhythmic passage, a musical *hook*.

Royalty: money paid for use of a song.

Song plugger: someone who promotes and pitches songs.

Staff producer: a producer contracted with a record company.

Staff writer: a songwriter who has signed an exclusive contract with a publisher.

Statutory rate: the mechanical royalty rate set by law (currently 6¼ percent pro rata of the retail price of a record) and specified in the mechanical licence.

Synchronisation ('sync') licence: a licence to synchronise a recording of a song with film or video tape.

Tracks: the separate parts a tape recorder can record at the same time (see Multitrack recording); the instrumental part of a recording as opposed to the vocal.

Verse: the part of a song that is usually repeated melodically, but with different lyrics each time.

INDEX

UNIVERSITY OF LIVERPOOL
DEPARTMENT OF CONTINUING EDUCATION LIBRARY

If you have enjoyed this book you will also be interested in the following Omnibus Press titles.

THE CRAFT OF LYRIC WRITING
Sheila Davis
ISBN: 0.7119.1718.3
Order No: OP 45152

MAKING MONEY MAKING MUSIC
James Dearing
ISBN: 0.7119.1721.3
Order No: OP 45186

THE SONGWRITER'S AND
MUSICIAN'S GUIDE TO MAKING
GREAT DEMOS
Harvey Rachlin
ISBN: 0.7119.1715.9
Order No: OP 45129

MAKING IT IN THE NEW MUSIC
BUSINESS
James Riordan
ISBN: 0.7119.1717.5
Order No: OP 45145

SUCCESSFUL LYRIC WRITING:
A STEP-BY-STEP COURSE &
WORKBOOK
Sheila Davis
ISBN: 0.7119.1720.5
Order No: OP 45178

PROFIT FROM YOUR MUSIC
James Gibson
ISBN: 0.7119.1716.7
Order No: OP 45137

GETTING NOTICED:
A MUSICIAN'S GUIDE TO
PUBLICITY & SELF-PROMOTION
James Gibson
ISBN: 0.7119.1719.1
Order No: OP 45160

HOW TO PITCH & PROMOTE YOUR
SONGS
Fred Koller
ISBN: 0.7119.1714.0
Order No: OP 45111

THE CRAFT & BUSINESS OF
SONGWRITING
John Braheny
ISBN: 0.7119.1820.1
Order No: OP 45418

BREAKS FOR YOUNG BANDS
Ed Berman
ISBN: 0.7119.0978.4
Order No: OP 43926

HOW TO MAKE AND SELL YOUR
OWN RECORD
Diane Sward Rapaport
ISBN: 0.7119.0759.5
Order No: AM 39785

HOW TO SUCCEED IN THE MUSIC
BUSINESS
Allan Dann & John Underwood
ISBN: 0.86001.454.1
Order No: AM 19977

THE PLATINUM RAINBOW:
HOW TO MAKE IT BIG IN THE
MUSIC BUSINESS
Bob Monaco & James Riordan
ISBN: 0.7119.1040.5
Order No: OP 44130

Omnibus Press
No. 1 for Rock & Pop Books